MONEY:

NATURE, HISTORY, USES, AND
RESPONSIBILITIES.

PHILADELPHIA:
AMERICAN SUNDAY-SCHOOL UNION,
NO. 146 CHESTNUT STREET.
LONDON:
RELIGIOUS TRACT SOCIETY.

NOTE.—The *American Sunday-school Union* have made an arrangement with the *London Religious Tract Society*, to publish, concurrently with them, such of their valuable works as are best suited to our circulation. In making the selection, reference will be had to the general utility of the volumes, and their sound moral tendency. They will occupy a distinct place on our catalogue, and will constitute a valuable addition to our stock of books for family and general reading.

As they will be, substantially, reprints of the London edition, the credit of their general character will belong to our English brethren, and not to us; and we may add, that the republication of them, under our joint imprint, involves us in no responsibility beyond that of a judicious selection. We cheerfully avail ourselves of this arrangement for giving wider influence and value to the labours of a sister institution so catholic in its character and so efficient in its operations as the *London Religious Tract Society*.

☞ The present volume is issued under the above arrangement.

CONTENTS.

CHAPTER I.

CHAPTER II.

CHAPTER III.

CHAPTER IV.

CHAPTER V.

CHAPTER VI.

APPENDIX.

MONEY.

CHAPTER I.

THE MONEY-MAKER: A SHORT LESSON IN SOCIAL ANATOMY.

THE subject of this little volume is MONEY; that powerful agent which sets in motion the various and complicated wheels of society, and without which the whole mighty machine would speedily come to a pause. Not less important also is the influence of money on individual interests. So greatly has it been prized by mankind, that it has even been boldly defined as an object, the possession or non-possession of which makes the difference whether life be an enjoyment or a task; whether it be a walk over a smooth verdant lawn amidst fragrant flowers and aromatic shrubs, or a wearisome journey through thorns and briers. Poets have sung, moralists have declaimed, and philosophers have speculated, respecting money. It is the object which has occupied the mind and enthralled the affections in all ages. Five thousand years have rolled along their course, but amidst the mighty alterations which the lapse of time has wrought, no abatement is witnessed in the eagerness with which the vast mass of mankind pursue money as the great object of life. Knowledge, however, has poured light upon this as upon all other subjects. If it has not led men to love money less than their forefathers did, it has at least enabled them better to understand the laws which regulate its production and distribution; it has shown also that although a power liable to great abuses, it deserves to be rescued from the indiscriminate denunciations in which some have indulged, and to be viewed in the light of a beneficial and social agent devised by God for the welfare of men.

It is not our intention, in the present treatise, to speak of money merely as it is known to our readers in the familiar shape of gold and silver coin, or bank notes. While largely adverting to these topics, we shall take, in their proper places, a more comprehensive view of the subject. It will be our aim accordingly to show, in a popular manner, the wisdom of the present constitution of society, of which money is the grand mainspring. We shall then endeavour to explain the mode in which that material wealth of which money is the representative is acquired. The history of gold, silver, and other symbols of value will next pass in review; the uses and abuses of money will be likewise noticed; and some examples will be furnished of men who largely benefited their day and generation by the right employment of this great talent. The philosophy, history, use, and abuse of money, form, in short, our theme.

We have said that money is the great motive power which sets in action the complicated wheels of society. It is necessary, however, to a full comprehension of this statement, that the principles upon which society has been framed by the all-wise Creator should be clearly understood, especially as very erroneous theories have been widely disseminated, not only on the continent but in our own country, upon the subject—theories which would discard the use of money, and propose as its substitute some wild and untried organizations of labour.

If these views were merely speculative we might pass them by without concern, but they are eminently practical, and if carried out would inflict enormous injury upon our social interests. They would cripple the money-making energies of the social system, and this we do not scruple to regard as one of the worst evils of a temporal kind which could befall us. When society is "making money," it is acquiring a larger stock of those things which add to the convenience and happiness of its members. Hence it is a serious thing when society ceases to grow rich. We may know then that the limit of future comfort is not far off, and that an epoch of privation is about to commence.

Society is often spoken of, in the language of personification, as a sentient being. This analogy is not altogether fanciful; there is much truth in it. Like the human body, it is endowed with " many members," each of which is fitted to discharge a distinct "office," while all are absolutely inter-dependent on each other. On examining our own physical constitution, we find it to be a most ingeniously constructed mechanism. The hand, the eye, and the ear, are marvels; so also are the blood-vessels and nerves, by means of which a constant and instantaneous communication is kept up with every corner of the system. But if we contemplate society with an eye to its internal arrangements, we shall be struck with *contrivances*, if we may so call them, equally remarkable. We see a vast array of different talents and employments, a wide labyrinth of passions and pursuits, all working together with a wonderful degree of harmony, each falling in with, and aiding the peculiar action of the rest. It is true we can also perceive here and there much that is unsightly and that betokens imperfect action; but this no more weakens the general impression of consummate design, than the diseases which sometimes disfigure the human body succeed in blinding our eyes to its admirable mechanism. In the human body, moreover, we are aware of the presence of something which we denominate LIFE, an energy distinct from physical organization, though closely connected with it, and on the maintenance of which the harmony and even the existence of the whole depends. Nothing in physical organization can compensate *the loss of life.* The hands may be exquisitely fashioned, every limb may have been cast in the most perfect mould, the face and head may rival in nobleness the inimitable sculptures of Canova; but let this inward energy expire, the embers of this mysterious fire die out, and ere long the whole will return to its original dust. So also, apart from the outward arrangements of society, we discern in it a principle of life which keeps the vast system stirring. Life is one of the grand features of society; we hear it in the rattle of our crowded streets, in the hum of the exchange, in the roar of the factory, in the shouts of its thousand operatives, in the shriek of the steam-engine, in the din of Billingsgate and Covent Garden, and the strange music of our "city cries." We see the same in the pressure of man on man in the pursuits of trade, in the eagerness of competition, the multiplicity of inventions, the rise of new professions in response to the call of newly developed wants, in the onward movement which carries society along with it to different, and almost always better conditions of existence. If we look within us we find the sources of this public life in the zest with which we give ourselves up to business, seeking at every step to make it the means of promoting the well-being of ourselves, and of those whom Providence has made dependent upon our exertions. Where these private impulses are most vigorous, as in Britain and the United States, society travels at the quickest pace, trades and manufactures are developed with the greatest energy, and a constant advance is made in civilization; but where these industrial impulses are weakest, as in Turkey, there society stands still, and ultimately falls to pieces.

We are justified, then, in regarding society as an organized body, pervaded by a vital force, upon the maintenance of which its functions and even its existence depend; but before proceeding to the inferences which such an illustration suggests, we will pause before one or two of the chief phenomena which society presents. The contemplation of these will show us the comparative excellence of its working, as well as the magnitude and responsibility of the task which those persons undertake who rashly propose to innovate in the very fundamentals of the social system.

One of the most remarkable facts which characterize the existing social system, is *the ease with which the diversified wants of large communities are met.* This involves an amount of individual distribution and combination which no degree of wisdom and energy could have arranged beforehand. How innumerable are our wants! Where shall we begin to reckon them? First in importance are those which relate to *subsistence.* What a quantity and variety of food do we require! Simple bread and water will not do. We must have food of a dozen different kinds and flavours; we must have the produce of the dairy, the garden, the vinery, the orchard; we must have tea and coffee, chocolate and spices, and our table must be occasionally replenished with oranges, raisins, tamarinds, and pine-apples. Next to food we must perhaps place *dress* and the *means of shelter*. Here, too, our wants, real and artificial, are all but numberless. Canvass, it is true, would answer the purposes of covering, and a blanket would furnish us with all the warmth we could desire ; but who would be content with these ? No ! our limbs must be wrapped in hose and flannel ; cotton must be covered, to suit our taste, with all the novelties of colour and design ; we must have linen and cloth and silk and fur ; grasses and gossamer must furnish an array for the head, while the hides of animals must yield a defence for the feet. To mention our houses is to add another legion to the catalogue of our wants: our chairs, tables, carpets, curtains, earthenware, pictures, glasses, musical instruments, besides the various articles required in the construction of the dwelling itself ; how many hands are needed to provide them ! In whatever other direction we look around, the prospect is equally boundless and diversified. It may safely be said that an English family of the middle class requires hundreds of separate professions in order to enjoy an average amount of the comforts and conveniences of life. And how different are these professions from each other ! How menial and laborious are some, how skilful and artistic are others ! How high do some stand in public estimation, how low do others fall ! Who shall decide which of these professions a man shall enter? Who shall guarantee that all shall be well supplied? Who shall arrange that all may work into each other's hands, so as to agree in time and place with the supply of our wants? It may be confidently affirmed that no amount of energy and forethought which has ever yet been found possessed by any man, or number of men, would be sufficient to do this. Yet how completely and regularly is it done for us! A vast population divides itself of its own accord into distinct groups, each of which forthwith enters upon some department of labour; the mine, the factory, the warehouse, the shop, each is filled with voluntary occupants, while others cross the seas to bring over the productions of other lands. Whenever a want is felt to a sufficient extent to produce a demand, then labourers at once are found, striving to furnish a supply. All this is done without coercion, without other than individual design; no central committee issues its decrees, no policeman is called in to enforce a theoretic organization of labour; every man is free to work or remain idle, and to work in just what sphere he pleases. How marvellous the law which thus reconciles the freedom of the individual with the welfare of the whole! What a striking display of Divine wisdom! How completely are the communistic inventions of modern times anticipated and outdone!

Social phenomena hardly less remarkable are seen in *the almost uniform price at which the same article can be purchased throughout an extensive district, and the general employment of the people in those departments of labour which are likely to yield most profit.* If we had to frame a social system, it would be most important to secure, by some means, both these objects. It would be unfortunate, if not unfair, for those who live in Lancashire to pay twice as much for the necessaries of life as the inhabitants of Kent and Devon. It would be difficult, perhaps impossible, to effect this equalization by any artificial plan, whereas it is accomplished with ease by individual enterprise, acting in obedience to the great law of supply and demand. The merchant wants to get the highest possible price for his commodities; this is in general the single point about which he troubles himself. It is nothing to him at what price they may ultimately be sold, nor what may suit the convenience of the people of London, Lancashire, or Devon; his anxiety is just to obtain as much as he can in return for his merchandise. But this mŏtive answers the purpose of the most profound combination and the most benevolent intentions. If his goods will fetch more a thousand miles off than they would at home, after deducting the expense of carriage, he will not hesitate to send them there. But if a considerable number of merchants, each acting on the same plan, send so many commodities to one place that its inhabitants have more than their proper share, the price will instantly fall as compared with that attainable at other markets, and the superabundance will soon be directed thither. Beautiful as the winding of a fertilizing stream is the course of the world's produce. Calmly it flows on in the path marked out for it by Providence, cheering now the rural hamlet, and anon spreading its beneficence in the heart of congregated thousands.

How important is it that the enterprise of a community should be directed into the most profitable channels! The working man understands this very well as applied to the narrower interests of home. He is well aware that the aggregate income and consequent condition of his family depend upon their being employed in that kind of labour in which the highest wages can be obtained, and he would count it ruinous to toil for ten shillings a week if, by turning his attention to something else, he could earn thirty. The *mode* in which he employs his labour evidently determines the comparative poverty or affluence in which he lives. All this is equally true of the entire commonwealth. It is of the utmost importance that the capital and labour of every community should be employed in those particular pursuits which will prove most lucrative; this is, indeed, decisive to a great extent of national prosperity or ruin. At the same time it is obvious that no artificial arrangements, no decrees of the state or the commune, would be able to accomplish this object; it would require an extent of knowledge, a depth of wisdom, and an array of coercive power, never yet beheld in combination. But what we could not secure by any artificial plan is arranged for us by Providence in the present constitution of society. The work is divided into an almost infinite number of shares, and each individual in entrusted with one. The entire community is probably making, under any given circumstances, the best possible use of its resources, since every member of the community is held by the strongest motives to make the best possible use of his own. In the busy world around us, every person is *on the look out* to improve his condition; to ascertain, namely, whether he can employ his labour more profitably. From the lowest grades of handicraft to the highest ranks of capital and skill, we find all animated with one desire. Is it a sinful or dishonourable desire? By no means. When properly regulated it is quite the opposite. We recognise in it one of those indications too often overlooked, which proclaim the footsteps of an almighty Architect.

We will select one more illustration of the working of our social system, and it shall be furnished by *the numerous instances of success in life which attract our attention on every hand.* Abused as this success may at times be, and too eagerly pursued as it is by some individuals, it yet forms an admirable arrangement of Providence for stimulating the active energies of the various individuals of which society is composed. We will take the pursuits of commerce and manufactures. What a multitude of striking facts meet us here! May it not be said without exaggeration, that we see around us a generation of princes whose fathers were peasants? Every valley of our manufacturing districts teems with traditions of successful industry. Everywhere individuals can be pointed out, now occupying the highest positions of social distinction, who once tended the loom, or whose parents were once the occupants of some humble cot which has since become a sort of rudely classic ground to the operative employed in the neighbouring factories. It is there told how one person who was raised some years ago to the magisterial bench, came into the district at first a poor youth from Scotland, carrying all his treasures in a handkerchief; and how, some forty years since, two brothers seated themselves on an eminence, which is now covered with a grove of dark pines and crowned with a handsome monument; ate their frugal meal—the purchase of their last penny, and surveyed the broad valley beneath, which was hereafter to become but a half of their ample possessions. Similar facts have become historic. A great man recently summoned away from us, whom history will place in the foremost rank of British statesmen, regarded it as an honour to call himself "the son of an Englishman, the founder of his own fortunes, by dint of honest and laborious exertion in the pursuits of active industry."* But it is not in one department alone that such instances of elevation have occurred; in science,

* Sir R. Peel's inaugural address at Glasgow.

literature, politics, and the legal profession we see the same; men who were once obscure, breaking their way through intervening obstacles to positions of reputation and influence; slowly but surely rising from the foremost class of some country grammar school to a seat in the cabinet, or a place on the judicial bench. Such posts, it is acknowledged, are seldom won without difficulty. In order to reach the goal, talents must be industriously developed, and circumstances promptly and perseveringly improved. But is this a disadvantage? None but those who join imbecility or indolence to ambition would think it so. Before we are permitted to grasp the prize it is well to be forced to work for it. The efforts occasioned by such a necessity are the costliest part of the reward. It is the discipline acquired in rising to greatness which fits the successful aspirant, with the grace of God, for standing on the giddy height. Here is, in fact, another proof of the Divine wisdom in the arrangements of society. If a man by some unexpected reverse or sudden process found himself placed at once in a position of great power, he would be very prone to arrogance and self-conceit; but when, as in the existing order of things, such a position can be reached only by a patient struggle with outward obstacles, and the diligent application of his personal talents, he acquires at the same time a certain moderation of spirit which is the true safeguard against the perils incident to an exalted station. It is also true that the number of those who succeed in realizing wealth and greatness can never be very large; the mass of mankind must always occupy a level far beneath. But it is also true that no man can rise by legitimate means without drawing others after him. All connected with him are the better for his elevation, and the greater the number of persons who attain to eminent success, the greater is the number of those who are partially successful; the success of a few raises the average well-being of all.

We have thus glanced at some of the more striking phases of the social system already presented to the reader's notice. We might adduce many more of the same character, but these will suffice to show the high degree of excellence which distinguishes the present constitution of society. The advantages we have contemplated are such as could not be dispensed with. If they were not enjoyed, communities could not exist. It is obvious, we think, that these benefits could not be secured by any artificial arrangements; the vast amount of contrivance, oversight, and authority, which would be required, is itself sufficient to render that impossible. The important objects we have considered must be secured by laws which influence the individual in his separate character, or not at all. Varied as these laws are, they may be all traced back to the operation of two simple principles—*the disposition which every person feels to promote his own interests; and the perfect right with which he feels himself invested to do this, provided only that he trench not on the equal rights of others.*

It were easy, did space permit, to vindicate these principles, and to show their superiority, especially when tempered by the precepts of Christianity, over those propounded by social theorists in our own day. But we have brought these questions before our readers merely as they are connected with *Money.* Money is the power which sets in motion the springs of action which we have now described, or, to vary the simile, it is the life blood which gives energy and warmth to the whole frame of the body corporate. Were society to be cast in the mould prescribed by the theories of Owen and others, money, it has been asserted, would no longer be required; but inextricable confusion, we may be assured, would inevitably follow any attempt to introduce a substitute for it.* As it now exists, money furnishes a short and admirable mode of distributing to each individual that exact portion of the wealth of society to which he can prove himself legitimately entitled; it is adapted alike to the largest and the minutest operations; (so marvellous and multifarious indeed is its agency, that it may be questioned which is more wonderful, the structure of society itself, or money, which gives vitality to its diversified operations.)

* The scenes of distress which occurred in Paris during the French revolution, when the government interfered with the purchase of bread, and distributed it in accordance with certain artificial regulations, powerfully illustrate the anarchy and confusion which would follow any attempt to do away with money as a distributory medium.

CHAPTER II.

MONEY-MAKING: HOW SOCIETY GETS RICH.

It is our object in the present chapter to show the mode in which society gradually becomes rich, and arrives at a state when the use of money as a circulating medium is required. This state of things is popularly supposed to be accomplished whenever a country abounds in gold and silver. We need hardly, however, remark that there is a certain amount of misapprehension on this view of the subject. A country may possess heaps of gold, and yet, in one sense, be poor; while another (as was the case with Scotland during the last century) may possess scarcely any bullion, and yet be rich in all that constitutes real material wealth. Gold and silver are, indeed—apart from their metallic uses — only the representatives of wealth; and in devoting our consideration, therefore, in the present chapter, to the mode in which society grows rich, we shall have to deal with a state of matters, much of which precedes the use of the precious metals in any form.

In contemplating society as it is exhibited in the history of mankind, we find it universally progressive. Sometimes this tendency has been manifested chiefly in a fruitless struggle with outward obstacles, and still oftener the process has been arrested in the lapse of centuries by some political catastrophe; but its existence is unquestionable. A number of emigrants fix upon some suitable spot as their future home: let us mark the result. Their stock consists at first merely of a few tools and weapons; these, and the strong arms which are prepared to wield them, are the young foundations of wealth and empire. Soon the forest resounds with the woodman's axe, and the first step is presently taken in the path to greatness; a village of mud cottages, interspersed with patches of cultivated land, which is covered, as autumn advances, with its first harvest. Visit the same spot after the lapse of fifty years: those rude huts have given way to streets of brick or stone; over the tops of the few trees which still remain as the hoary representatives of a fallen dynasty, the domes and turrets of civic structures meet the eye, while all around we see the fruits of industry in a profusion of gardens, orchards, corn-fields, and meadow-lands. Let another half century pass by, and what see we now? A spacious city, a very mart of commerce, the floor of whose exchange is trodden by merchants from every clime. Wherever we turn, our attention is attracted by objects of public interest, from countless mast-heads we see waving the colours of all nations, while our ears are incessantly dinned with the noise of the steam-engine or the rattle of the loom. The houses of the wealthy abound in evidences of intelligence and taste, and even the poorest—survey his cottage, examine his stock of food and clothing, and then say how much better is he off than the best of those poor wanderers who cleared the first acre, and ate their first thrifty meal beneath the shelter of a wattled cabin.

This is the process which has taken place wherever men have dwelt together, from the time when "Asshur went forth and builded Nineveh," down to the latest settlement among the prairies of the "far west." Wherever intelligence and industry join hands, a career of prosperity commences, something is continually won from the earth over and above what is required for present wants; this serves as a stepping-stone to a still greater surplus, which becomes in time productive of one still greater. Not only does wealth increase, but a corresponding expansion takes place in the physical and intellectual resources of the state; science, philosophy, literature, and art exhibit the signs of regular and rapid growth. Discovery succeeds discovery, and every day renders all natural resources more completely subservient to the wants of man ; splendour rears its halls and palaces, sculpture moulds its monuments and statues, while poetry diffuses all around the harmonies of song. If we compare man as he appears in this advanced stage of civilization with his former self, when he reared his hut on the edge of the forest, we experience the same impressions as when the eye passes from the sapling oak of yesterday to the still blooming veteran of a thousand winters. We feel that a glorious creation has slowly acquired birth and being—a creation finer, perhaps, even than the old mountains and bottomless seas; a commonwealth of men, a congress of kings; and this result has been attained, not by theory, not by a laborious induction of facts, not by adopting any artificial system, not even by aiming deliberately at its accomplishment, but simply by obeying the practical impulses with which the human bosom is inspired.

But some would deny that a highly civilized condition is either the happiest or the most natural to man. The savage state is lauded as preferable to ours, or at least that normal stage of civilization when women were all clad in russet and men in "sober grey;" when, according to a pleasant fiction, all had enough, and none had anything to spare; when architecture soared no higher than the thatched cottage, and mankind seemed as if they begged permission to "squat" upon the earth's surface, instead of grasping its dominion with a master's hand. To this we reply, that whatever attractions such a state may seem to wear, it is indebted for them exclusively to our own fancy. This faculty is sufficiently affluent to connect ideas of romance with a company of naked savages, and construct an arcadian republic out of tomahawks and wigwams. But such conceptions are merely poetic dreams. Man, in an uncivilized state, is ignorant, sensual, superstitious, and we know that such qualities cannot comport with happiness. Equally groundless is the supposition that in a savage state the wants and resources of mankind were ever accurately balanced. It might, perhaps, be safely asserted, that the possession of a bare competence is only possible when society has become civilized. Society itself never pauses, it always fluctuates between progress and decay, and those principles which do not lead to wealth, will soon plunge it in poverty. Five hundred years ago, England was incomparably poorer than it is at present, but it does not appear that the struggle for subsistence was the less arduous. The poor man found as much labour required to feed his children with beans and barley as the factory operative experiences in providing his family with the finest wheaten flour. The hardest day's work an Englishman is required to undergo, and for which he is remunerated with a thousand domestic comforts, is not half so hard as that which barely suffices to keep the North American Indian above the point of absolute starvation. Still less can it be said that such a primitive state is natural to man. A state of nature, when man is the theme, is not composed of nakedness, ignorance, penury, and brutal coarseness. It might be so if, as some philosophers have thought, the progenitors of the human race crawled out of the ground like snails, or made their way up to humanity through a dreary set of piscatory and apish transmigrations. It would then be reasonable to suppose that their first scale of living was not much higher than the beaver's, though even on this supposition it would not follow that any stage of improvement, short of the very highest, is his final goal. But the circumstances which attended man's introduction to his earthly abode were so refined, that a savage state could never be anything but an unspeakable degradation, an unnatural state, which he was bound, as soon as possible, to quit for ever. On looking back, we obtain in Paradise a faint glimpse of our true social elevation. Then man was happy, his mental faculties vigorous, and his outward condition all that could be desired. Civilization came, arrayed in her native radiance, and lavished her treasures on the holy pair. True, sin poured its vial on the lovely scene, and our next glimpse of man presents him to us in a sadly altered state; but his natural elevation is still that of his earliest days, which, by a long redemptive process, must be reached again. Hence every department of human progress is beheld centering in the same design; the consolidation of society, the growth of wealth, the cultivation of science and art, combine with the specific influences of Christianity in restoring man to that which alone can be regarded as his proper and natural condition; in raising the entire race to that pitch of moral and physical perfection which marked the commencement of its career.

The first step in the acquisition of wealth is *a recognition of the rights of property.* These rights are not factitious; they do not exist by virtue of any social compact; they are inherent in our nature, and all they ask from us is a recognition of their validity. No doctrine in the compass of social science is more important than this. It is the key-stone of the arch which conducts us across the foaming abyss of chaos, and lands us on the rock of order. Deny these rights, and society falls to pieces; admit them, and little more than their consistent application is required to raise it to the highest state of material well-being.

A recognition of the rights of property tends to the acquisition of wealth, by insuring to every man the fruits of his own labour. Self-interest is the mainspring of social life. The mechanic, the merchant, the capitalist all agree in this, each consults his own welfare, each asks, "What will be most profitable to myself?" and this determines the fate of every transaction. All the exchanges at this moment taking place in the various marts of Europe, have been arranged in the full confidence that they will prove advantageous to both the parties concerned, and a reasonable doubt of this on either side would have prevented them from being made. In contemplating the movements of self-interest, we stand in the engine-house of the world, and behold the power which moves a large portion of the machinery of human affairs. It is not our object now to vindicate this principle; we believe it, as we have before said, when regulated by Christian principle, to be legitimate and most beneficent: but let us simply look to facts. What merchant would sit up early and late in his counting-house if he knew that at the year's end he was not to have the disposal of the fruits of his toil? What operative would rise cheerfully at the sound of the factory bell, stint his meal hours, and perhaps work on till near midnight, if he had no hope of receiving proportionably higher wages? What prudent farmer would spend all his capital in improving his land, if he knew he should be deprived of it at the next rent-day? Such conduct would, under ordinary circumstances, be in the highest degree unreasonable.

Since the chief motive to labour arises from the prospect of owning its results, whatever tends to promote the security of property may be regarded as a source of wealth. The stronger the guarantee afforded that whoever expends his labour in any enterprise shall reap its fruits, the likelier is it that society will grow richer. To the superior stability of every species of right in free states may we ascribe the commercial eminence they have generally attained. Enterprise shrinks into inactivity beneath the touch of despotic power. Naboth's vineyard was lost when it attracted the cupidity of Ahab; and it is mentioned as a rare instance of magnanimity in an absolute sovereign that Frederic the Great of Prussia permitted a windmill to stand within sight of the royal palace, out of deference to the owner. The peasantry of Wallachia are said to exist in a state of the most abject wretchedness, and yet it is believed that most of them have a hoard of gold in the vicinity of their dwellings. They are driven to wear this show of poverty by the extortionate conduct of their governors, whose tenure of office depends upon the amount of money they are able to wring from the people. It is instructive to reflect that, while money is thus suffered to lie unproductive beneath the soil, the Danube, which flows in the immediate neighbourhood, is almost unnavigable for want of capital. But it is not political corruption alone which, by rendering property insecure, prevents the acquisition of wealth ; faction, revolutions, wars, crime, will produce the same effect. So also will those social arrangements which prevent the outlay of capital, by withholding proper security for its remuneration.

After the rights of property have been recognised, the next step in the acquisition of wealth is *the appropriation of the soil.* It has been found that wherever the land is held in common, no considerable improvement takes place in the condition of the people. Tribes who depend for their subsistence upon the earth's raw produce, retain the same savage character for ages; while those who settle upon and cultivate some one spot soon become civilized. The New Englander enjoyed no advantage over the aboriginal tribes of North America; the climate and geographical peculiarities of the country were the same to all: yet while our Anglo-Saxon brethren have grown in two centuries to the proportions of a great nation, the native population has become all but extinct. One reason of this is obvious. The Saxon proceeded at once to a division of the land, giving every man a fixed portion to possess and cultivate, while the Indian still retains the nomadic habits of his ancestors. A country whose inhabitants subsist on its spontaneous produce, must be very thinly peopled. This single fact is full of gloomy inferences. Scarcely any intercourse can take place among such a people; the very law of their existence is separation, the presence of any considerable number at the same spot being absolutely forbidden by the capacities of the soil. Thus forcibly held asunder, they soon become positively hostile to each other; strangers to the cementing influence of fellowship in productive industry, they resemble two beasts of prey contending for the same heap of offal. But these evils are not the worst; we discover a truly tragic depth of misery in the necessity which exists for a constant curtailment of the population, so as to keep it within the limits fixed by a scarcity of food, for it is well remarked by Adam Smith, that although poverty tends, in the first instance, to multiply rather than diminish the human species, yet it is extremely unfavourable to the rearing of them to maturity. The thinness of the population in a poor country proves, not that fewer in proportion are born, but that a greater number die.

The importance of the appropriation of the soil, considered as a step in social progress, springs from the fact that all our wealth is derived ultimately from this source. The most necessary articles of subsistence, such as wheat, rice, and potatoes, are the immediate fruits of agriculture. Good pasturage is necessary to supply us with milk, cheese, and the various kinds of animal food. We should soon have no skins, no leather, no woollen clothing, no beasts of burden, if there were no vegetable produce. Flax, cotton, tea, coffee, are derived from the same source, and without the mulberry-tree the silkworm would soon perish. The most splendid furniture with which our drawing-rooms are adorned, may be traced to its home in the forest or the mine; our fairest crystals once lay hid in the obscurity of sand and rock. Even the treasures of genius, themselves drawn from a higher source, must be un-hoarded by earthen instruments. The poet's pen was once a goose's quill, the artist's pencil is drawn from the camel's hide; and the very material to whose care the painter consigns his imperishable productions once waved in the cotton-fields of Georgia, or gambolled on a sheep's back among sunshine and flowers. Imagine these varied gifts of the earth withdrawn, and how wretched would our condition become! But trace them to their home, and we find them all springing from the application of labour to the soil under the law of self-interest. The world's market is stocked with wealth, because some millions of landowners find it profitable to develop the capabilities of the soil. But let all appropriation cease, and every portion of it be as much the property of one man as another, and all activity would cease too ; we should sink from wealth to competence, from competence to scarcity, and from scarcity to ruin.

Next to the recognition of the rights of property, and the appropriation of the soil, the most important step in the acquisition of wealth is *the division of labour*. The first guarantees the enjoyment of the fruits of labour, the second converts into property the material to which labour is applied, while the third increases the productiveness of labour itself. Dr. Adam Smith ascribes the discovery of the principle of divided labour to the advantages which men would soon experience in confining their attention to one kind of work. Archbishop Whately objects to this view, that it accounts for the continued application of the principle, but not for its first adoption, and traces the arrangement to its being found that many operations of the same kind could be carried on at the same time, and by the same means. Thus a person who had occasion to fetch a bucket of water from the spring could carry two buckets with little additional trouble. A courier between two towns could convey two hundred letters almost as easily as one. If a man required a few wooden pales in order to fence his garden, he would find that when the tree was cut down and severed in the required lengths, it would cost him comparatively little more trouble to supply his neighbour with the same article. Thus the principle could not fail to be discovered at the very outset of civilization, and when once discovered it was too valuable a boon to throw away.

The increased productiveness of labour through the distribution of its various branches among as many different workmen, arises, according to Adam Smith, from the superior dexterity which a person soon acquires when he confines himself exclusively to one set of operations, from the time which is saved by keeping to the same routine of work, and the greater inventiveness which is produced by directing the attention chiefly to one department. A single pin is valueless to a proverb, yet on its way to the toilet it passes through eighteen distinct processes, each of which in large manufactories, is a separate branch of labour, and the cost of production is diminished by this means more than two hundred and fifty times. The vast increase of wealth and convenience which may be ascribed to the adoption of this simple principle is beyond conception. If the reader happens to be a lady, will she reflect a moment upon the history of the material which sometimes constitutes her morning dress? That fine cotton fabric could only have been produced by the labour of thousands. How many were employed in cultivating the original plant; in sowing, tending, picking it, and at last shipping its produce to the ports of Europe. The ship which brought it over the Atlantic is itself the representative of a series of distinct trades, including the woodman, the miner, the nailer, the carpenter, the rope-maker, and the weaver. From the merchant's warehouse to the draper's shop how many metamorphoses did the cotton undergo? Two or three preparatory dressings, as many sets of spinners, then the weaver, bleacher, and calico-printer. But each of these includes in itself a crowd of distinct professions. What a complication of contrivances is the mechanism employed, from the steam-engine to the spinning-jenny, the loom and the printing-machine! What a history might be written on the various chemical processes alone; the preparation of the mordants, the procuring of the drugs, and the mixing of the colours! How many designers are employed to sketch those elegant patterns which often hold the fair purchaser in suspense between equal beauties, and how much skilled labour is required to transfer those patterns to the wooden block or the copper roller, before they can be stamped upon the cloth! A curious instance of the numerous processes required to bring to perfection some articles of mere luxury is found in the history of the more expensive kinds of tobacco pipes. The material itself, which is called *écume de mer*, is a kind of fuller's earth from the south of Crim Tartary. The first rude shape is given to the pipes on the ground where the material is first dug, by pressing them into a mould, and leaving them to harden in the sun. They are then baked in an oven, boiled in milk, and rubbed with soft leather. In this state they are taken to Constantinople, where they are bought by merchants, and sent in caravans to Pesh, in Hungary. They are then soaked for twenty-four hours in water, after which they are turned upon a lathe. From Pesh they are taken to Vienna, whence they are distributed through the markets of Germany.

If a person who makes two blades of grass grow where only one grew before, adds to the riches of mankind, how large an accession of wealth is due to an arrangement which makes labour many hundred times more productive than it would have been without it! That this arrangement *does* increase the productiveness of labour is unquestionable. If every man had to make his own clothes, graze his own cattle, kill his own meat, how heavy and slow would be the progress of society! We do that best and quickest which we do oftenest. But not only is increased facility the result of the division of labour; by concentrating our attention on one process we discern more easily new and better ways of doing it. Hence the use of machinery may be ascribed to the same principle. Let no one think otherwise of this than of a great blessing; so long as it is not labour that man wants, but the fruits of labour, whatever increases the productiveness of labour must be a benefit to mankind, since it must tend either to multiply their comforts or diminish their toil. An objection has been urged against the division of labour that, by simplifying the work of the operative, it makes him a mere machine, and weakens his intellectual powers by not calling them into exercise. In our opinion such an objection is groundless. We may rest assured that the mind will always find something to do. The simpler the work on which a man is employed, the more freely may he allow his mind to revert to other and more pleasing topics, and the greater the mental elasticity he will carry into his leisure hours. A person whose sole employment during twelve hours has been to see that a machine does its work properly, must be in a far better condition for spending an hour at night over some bracing book than if he had performed that work himself. Besides, there can be no antagonism between good tendencies. If the instrument to which we are mainly indebted for our social comforts becomes, in proportion to its perfectness, the means of intellectual annihilation to those who employ it, where would be the wisdom of the social architect? But experience confutes the objection. We venture to say that there is not a more intelligent body of operatives in the world than that part of the population of Lancashire and Yorkshire which is engaged in the cotton and woollen manufactures; while farm-labourers, whose occupations exemplify, on the authority of Adam Smith, the division of labour to the least possible extent, have always been reckoned to be, as a body, inferior in *point of mental activity* to the mechanics of our large towns. Should it be said that this superiority is owing, not to the division of labour, but to the better opportunities of mental culture afforded in our large towns, we reply that large towns themselves, with their numberless appliances of civilization, are the offspring of this very principle, and that we find here an additional proof that the conditions of wealth and popular intelligence are not opposed, but are invariably and indissolubly one.

The division of labour leads at once to *exchange.* When every person provided in the best way he could for his own wants, he had no occasion to barter with his neighbour. His condition might not be one of comfort, but it was at least one of independence. As soon, however, as each confined himself to one depart ment of labour, his independence was at an end. Very few of his personal wants could be supplied by his own exertions, and for the rest he would have to seek the co-operation of others. The smith, for instance, who worked all day long at his forge, would make many more nails than he would require for his own use, but he would stand in need of food and clothing, articles which could not be produced within the walls of his smithy. The farmer, the butcher, the grocer, would each find himself in a similar position; they would respectively have more grain, more meat, and more sugar than they would be able to consume themselves, while each would stand in need of what the others could supply. In these circumstances exchange would naturally take place. This process, however, is merely a matter of convenience. It does not increase the aggregate results of labour; it simply affects their ownership, but at the same time it developes a new principle which occasions a positive increase of wealth. It is plain that, since all wealth is the produce of labour, the productiveness of labour is just the measure of wealth, and whatever insures that labour shall always be expended so as to be most productive must be a valuable aid to social progress. This useful principle is competition. This principle, though acting with the greatest force in the most civilized communities, must have exerted a powerful influence even in the earliest times. Things soon began to be distinguished as cheap or dear, and traders instinctively exercised their prerogative of carrying their commodities where they would fetch the most. If it were not for this wholesome check, no prudential obligations would lie upon the producer. He might turn his attention to pursuits for which he had no natural aptitude; he would have no powerful motive to economy, industry, and self-culture; secure of a market whatever the quality or the amount of his own exertions, he would soon become careless and inactive. On such a system we should have no guarantee that society put forth one-half its energies, or that the energy it actually put forth was not wasted by being misapplied. Competition renders these evils impossible. Its tendency is twofold—to force both individuals and nations into those departments of effort for which they are most fitted, and to compel them to put forth the largest possible amount of skill and labour. Such coercion may not be altogether pleasant, but it is salutary; as much so for the individual as for the state.

A crusade has been waged for some time past, with a considerable measure of popular applause, against the principle of competition, and clamorous demands are made, not only in our own country, but on the continent, for its exclusion from the social code. No doubt competition is a principle which requires to be regulated by Christian maxims; we but must demur to the propriety or even the possibility of complying with the above demand. The most direct way of acceding to it would be to fix the lowest price at which articles shall be sold; but what would be the effect of such a step? It would certainly enable the imprudent or inferior tradesman to sell his goods at more than their natural price, but the difference would be so much abstracted from the pocket of the purchaser. Not only would he have to pay more, but the extra price would indicate a corresponding amount of clear loss in the aggregate amount of social wealth, inasmuch as fewer inducements would be held out to ingenuity and effort. If such an arrangement were adopted in one trade, it ought to be allowed in all. The most incompetent craftsman ought to be allowed the privilege of fixing the exchangeable value of his productions. But it is plain that this would be a system of virtual pauperism, and that society would thus inflict upon itself a huge tax on behalf of those who least deserved such a boon.

But instead of fixing the price of commodities, a more complicated expedient has been proposed. It has been suggested that, instead of each endeavouring to surpass the rest, all should work in common, contributing to, and drawing upon, a common fund. This is pure socialism, the principles of which we have before noticed, and little danger need be apprehended from such a source. The principle which is now opposed to competition is *co-operation*, and to this our remarks will be confined. The co-operative theory, if we may judge from recent experiments, is altogether distinct from socialism, and ought not to assume the same name. A number of individuals belonging to a common profession agree to raise money among themselves, or on mutual credit, with a view to engage in business on their own account. Such an association may be somewhat novel in its aim, but the principle on which it is founded has been carried out in numberless instances by individuals who would have repudiated any approximation to socialism. It is, in fact, a joint-stock company, the members of which agree to work themselves, and so secure double profits. It is a mistake, however, to speak of co-operation and competition as things opposed. Competition is thoroughly co-operative, and the success of co-operation depends upon its being thoroughly competitive. A firm composed of fifty partners act as much on the principle of competition as if there were only two. Among themselves they are co-operative, but the point at which they dovetail with society is and must be competitive. If, therefore, society can be rescued from its miseries only by putting down competition, it is evident that co-operative associations do not touch the case.

To co-operative associations thus simply constituted, and resting for success entirely upon the excellence and cheapness of their productions, no objection, as far as principle is concerned, can be preferred. The chief effect of such associations would be to add so many more to the existing number of competitors, and thus increase the severity of competition. But one all-important question yet remains,—Will they answer? The prudential test is the only one which can be properly applied, but this, we fear, must prove decisive. Destitute of special privileges, forced to obey the inexorable laws of political economy, it is difficult to imagine how they can succeed, considering the peculiar perils to which they are exposed. Either the adoption of a too popular basis will prevent business being transacted with the requisite measure of rapidity and precision, or else the entire concern will be left to the discretion of a few individuals, in which case it will insensibly slide into their own hands. If we may take one with which we were to some extent personally acquainted as an illustration of the manner in which all are carried on, our hopes of their success would be far from sanguine. Every question was there settled by "universal suffrage," a principle which, whatever it may be in politics, is obviously inapplicable to business. Not a farthing was disposed of without putting it to the test of a lengthy discussion; and very often, before the members determined what course to take, the time for action had gone by. It was also painful to mark a jealousy of superior abilities, and a preference, in making official appointments, for men whom the rest could easily "manage," rather than those whose talents would be likely to insure success. Those members of the society whose intellects were not the brightest, were apt to imagine that a plot lay hid beneath every proposal they could not comprehend, yet still, tenacious of their rights as partners, they were determined that no measure should be adopted which did not force their assent, and thus they became a mere set of "obstructives." An intelligent and highly skilled mechanic, who once belonged to the association adverted to, assured us that if his own business were carried out on the same principles, it would not be worth a shilling in six months.

The last step in the progress of wealth

is *international commerce.* The immediate occasion of this is found in the difference which exists between the productions of various climes, and their general suitableness to the use of man. Perhaps no two soils can be found which, in return for the same amount of labour, bring forth the same article in the same degree of perfection. Countries consisting of low alluvial plains find pasturage most profitable; those which enjoy a dry soil and clear atmosphere abound in grain. Some situations are peculiarly favourable to the vine; others to flax, cotton, or the sugar-cane; while others, owing to their mineral treasures and peculiar geographical advantages, are most suited to manufactures. While the productions of different nations are so various, all men have nearly the same wants. The tea which pleases the Chinaman is a luxury in Britain; while our cutlery, earthenware, and textile produce find a ready market in any part of the earth. Providence seems by this arrangement to have provided for the friendly intercourse of mankind, and in proportion as it has been recognised and carried out have the best interests of mankind been promoted. The tendency of commerce is to diminish the frequency of war, and, next to the special influences of the gospel, is the most powerful agent in the work of civilizing the globe.

The pecuniary advantages of commerce consist in its enabling us to exchange articles which cost us little labour for others which though perhaps equally inexpensive in the country where they were produced, would require here a much larger outlay; and when two nations mutually exchange their cheapest productions for those which, if produced at home, would be the dearest, the greatest possible addition is made in that instance to the wealth of the world. This statement admits of a simple illustration. It is well known that oranges are imported in large quantities into this country from Spain and Portugal; but it is not impossible to grow oranges here at home. By special care they may readily be produced in hot-houses, as the gardens of our nobility attest; but as they cannot be produced at home at nearly so low a rate as that at which they can be imported, their domestic cultivation is confined to the purposes of horticultural science. If they could not be produced at home for less than twopence a piece, while at Seville they could be purchased for a halfpenny, and the expense of their carriage would not be more than their original cost, it is evident that by going to a foreign market we should effect a saving to the amount of one-half. If we had previously expended half a million annually in the growth of oranges, we should, by turning importers, save £250,000, and should be richer to precisely that amount. But it may happen that at Seville, while oranges are cheap, cotton cloth is dear. By manufacturing the article at home it might cost them twenty shillings a piece, while we could afford to let them have it for one-fourth of that sum. Hence, instead of receiving payment for their oranges in money, they would find it more advantageous to take the amount in goods of that description. These might be sold in Seville at least fifty per cent. cheaper than the home manufacture, and would involve a clear saving of one-half their annual outlay in cotton goods. Thus, in commerce, both parties are benefited, and their joint profits represent the clear increase which it contributes to the aggregate wealth of mankind.

From the very earliest times it has been the practice of nations to exchange with each other. The silver with which Abraham bought the field and cave of Machpelah is called "current money of the merchant;" and the Ishmaelites, to whom Joseph was sold, were carrying spices into Egypt. As exchange is mutually profitable, separation is the chief hindrance to commerce, and hence camels and ships were always its efficient promoters, the former bridging the desert, and the latter the sea. The Phœnicians were the navigators and merchants of the old world; they were carriers and barterers for all nations. Tyre and Sidon were flourishing commercial cities in the time of Solomon, and both seem to have engaged with that monarch in several commercial enterprises. The celebrated Tadmor, whose ruins still prolong something of its former magnificence, was probably built with the view of promoting the caravan trade between Palestine and the Persian Gulf. From Eziongeber, a port on the Red Sea, a fleet, conducted by Syrian navigators, sailed to Ophir and Tarshish, and brought back to Solomon and the king of Tyre apes, ivory, peacocks, and gold. It is thought that the Hebrew term *bedil*, in the book of Numbers, should be rendered *tin*. The "brass" which was employed in making the utensils of Solomon's temple, like that which was extensively used among the Greeks, was in reality bronze, or a mixture of iron and tin; but this latter metal the ancients obtained exclusively from Spain or the British Isles. The Romans were never a mercantile people, and, with the exception of Alexandria, no city appears to have risen to special commercial eminence, till Venice rose amidst the waters of the Adriatic. The Crusades stimulated the desire for intercourse with the east, and poured a golden tide into the coffers of the wary merchants of St. Mark. Then, as in olden times, the treasures of India were brought to the shores of the Mediterranean, from whence they were carried by the Venetian ships to the various markets of Western Europe. The discovery of America in the fifteenth century opened a new field for commercial enterprise, and the discovery of the route to India by the Cape of Good Hope, transferred for a time the commercial sceptre to the Portuguese. On the emancipation of the Netherlands from the Spanish yoke, the flame of commercial enterprise burst forth in the United Provinces.

The Dutch flag waved on the shores of Africa, Asia, and the new world, but in its turn drooped before the one which since has known no rival. Our country has long been the commercial metropolis of the globe; our ships are carriers for the world; a large proportion of the aggregate merchandise of mankind is carried in British vessels; our manufacturing energy, seeking an outlet for itself, has opened channels of intercourse with the most distant and barbarous lands. But we would not wish, if it were possible, to be alone in this magnificent work. Our brethren of the United States, true to their origin, and backed by natural resources in some respects superior to our own, will soon be by our side. Let both welcome each other to the post of honour, and inscribe on the flag which they jointly bear in the van of the world's progress—"ONE—INDISSOLUBLY ONE—IN JUSTICE AND LOVE FOR EVER."

CHAPTER III.

THE CHEMISTRY OF MONEY: A FEW WORDS ABOUT CAPITAL.

We have considered in their natural order of development the various steps which lead to the acquisition of wealth: we now proceed to consider the same subject in another and still more interesting point of view; with regard, namely, to the two co-efficients which always concur in its production. Capital and labour may be regarded as twin powers, born at the same moment, gifted with the same length of existence, fitted to accomplish in concert what neither could possibly accomplish by itself. So far from being opposed, they are necessarily co-operative, and whatever fluctuations await them in society, they must live or die together. Labour is the parent of capital, and capital is the soul of labour. Destroy either, and the acquisition of wealth becomes a vanishing dream.

1. What is capital? We will suppose a number of persons intent upon reclaiming fifty or sixty acres of that boggy land which abounds in the west of Ireland. The task we shall

suppose is considered practicable. Appropriate manures are abundant and within easy reach. A certain method of procedure will assuredly bring this wet and rotten soil into a condition fit for bearing the best produce. But twelve months must pass away before any results can be obtained, and several years before the projectors' expectations can be fully realized. How then shall the persons be sustained in the meantime? Their families will daily need food and clothing, they themselves will require tools to work with, as well as horses and carts for the conveyance of soil. The ground, as it is reclaimed, must be fenced off, and superfluous moisture carried away by means of drainage. It is certain that, how profitable soever the enterprise might prove, until these resources are provided from some quarter, it cannot possibly be undertaken. Labourers may offer themselves by thousands, some such employment may be their only refuge from absolute starvation; but the condition is imperative—some person must find them implements and food; deny this and they may perish in the midst of natural affluence. The necessity for capital is still more evident in the case of manufactures, since here it is requisite to provide materials as well as tools and sustenance. To-morrow morning a hundred thousand persons will proceed to the factories of Manchester; but what would they do if, on reaching their respective places of employment, they found no employer to receive them, no materials, no machines, no workshops? Perhaps their first impulse would be to commence working for themselves; but how many obstacles would rise in opposition to this design! Factories must be erected, materials purchased, and costly machines set up. When their ingenuity and labour had converted these raw materials into useful articles, they would be no nearer the end of their exertions till money or other commodities had been procured in exchange. Even this might not prove a very easy matter. No doubt articles of real utility may generally be sold at some price, but there are seasons when this price would do no more than defray the cost of material, if it did even that, leaving nothing for the labourer; and goods, if they are to remunerate the owner, must be kept back to await a higher demand. Hence labour is useless without some fund out of which the labourer can be provided with tools and materials, as well as sustenance for himself and family, till his labour has actually become productive; and everything which fur nishes those resources, everything which is employed in setting the labourer to work, whether it is *fixed* in buildings and machinery, or *floating* in the shape of money between manufacturer and merchant, master and man, is called CAPITAL.

2. Let us now ask, How is capital produced? The original source to which the production of capital must be ascribed, is the liberal return which, in the arrangements of our Creator, the earth makes to any one who bestows labour upon it Referring to the illus-

tration already adduced, if the produce of fifty acres, which we supposed a number of persons to be bent upon reclaiming from the bogs of Ireland, was only sufficient to replace, without surplus, what had actually been expended in raising it, those persons would necessarily be obliged to confine their efforts to the quantity of land at first inclosed. Twelve months' produce being only able to keep them during an equal period, they would live, to use an expressive saying, from hand to mouth, with nothing to spare. If this had been the case universally, not only could mankind never have grown rich, but if the present laws which regulate the increase of the human race had been in force, they must always have pined in misery, since there never could have been any surplus on which to maintain families, or maintain the labourer till his labour became remunerative. But Providence has ordained a very different state of things. The produce of fifty acres is found sufficient not only to cover the cost of production, but to furnish a wide margin of profits. Our Irish cultivators would find themselves at the year's end not only repaid for the money which had been expended in food, clothing, and implements, but possessed of a considerable quantity of commodities to be disposed of as they saw fit. They might now look beyond their fifty acres; having saved enough to support several additional labourers during the next twelve months, they might now inclose a larger plot of ground, of which, at the end of the year, they would naturally possess the profits. It is plain that no limits need be set to such a process but those which spring from the capabilities of the soil. They might go on, bringing district after district into cultivation, till their farms inclosed all the waste land in the country. The annual surplus might then be turned into other channels, employed in shipping, mining, manufactures, or any other remunerative pursuit, the aggregate amount always increasing, and its capacities accordingly always becoming greater. All existing capital arose in this manner. It was at one time or other *saved* out of the results of labour and previous capital, and the earliest capital was that which God provided in the spontaneous productions of the earth which sustained a spare population during the first operations of agriculture.

Capital thus springs originally from the prolific abundance of the earth's natural resources—from the goodness of the Creator, who has ordained that wherever man puts forth his five talents they shall presently be increased to ten. It is useful, however, to regard it as *savings*, as the excess of income beyond expenditure, since the production of capital is thus exhibited in connexion with our own personal efforts. When, in a primitive state of society, the husbandman, after replacing the corn and clothing required while awaiting the harvest, found sufficient grain in his storehouse to supply the wants of the coming season, he had so much capital; and if the mechanic who receives twenty shillings weekly manages to put by two shillings out of that sum, he adds by so much to the national capital; his weekly savings increase the fund which can be employed in the remuneration of labour. Every properly economical act has the same tendency. Every farthing legitimately rescued from expenditure helps to provide a fund from which may be drawn the means of more largely increasing trade, and raising the demand for labour; and money, however invested, whether in building clubs, freehold land societies, an insurance office, or the savings' bank, becomes an efficient servant to the commonwealth. Those institutions do not suffer it to lie idle; it is at once put out to the most profitable use, that in which it will, in its turn, yield the largest increase to existing capital.

3. We have seen that capital thus produced has a natural tendency to accumulate; let us glance at the chief circumstances which favour or retard its accumulation. One point most essential to the accumulation of capital is the supply of cheap materials. Other things being equal, a country where the raw staple of manufactures is most abundant must beat its neighbours in the chase of wealth. It seldom happens, however, that this equality exists. We see here one of the many proofs of a harmony of interests pervading the entire conditions of humanity. Raw materials being generally the products of agriculture, are cheapest in a

country but thinly populated. There, however, skilled labour is the dearest. In a populous country, on the other hand, labour is comparatively cheap, but raw materials are dear. Thus, in the United States cotton must be cheaper by the cost of carriage than it is at Liverpool; but the superior cheapness of labour in this country nevertheless enables us to manufacture cotton goods at less cost than the Americans.

Equal in importance with cheap material is the natural price of labour, that price which capital can afford to pay and yet remain profitable. This price is regulated by laws as fixed as those which determine the relation of electricity and thunder, or the flow and ebb of the tides. Labour, like every other commodity, like capital itself, finds its own level. Any attempt, by artificial means, to raise it above tnat point is as unwise as to resolve that water shall not freeze when its temperature sinks below freezing-point. When wages *can* ascend above any given rate they necessarily *will* ascend above it, and the attempts to prevent this would be as futile as to stop the progress of the tides. Strikes are not necessary to ascertain the proper price of labour. When capital can afford higher wages, it soon becomes its interest to offer them. It would, too, be well if the forcible measures which are frequently put in operation to raise wages were simply unsuccessful, but in proportion as they are persevered in they cripple capital; they diminish the only fund which can pay wages, and the entire carrying out of the theory on which they are based would consummate the ruin of trade, and the commercial downfall of the country. Our prosperity is not guaranteed us by any special law. Amidst the competition of nations we have kept uppermost, but we have no exclusive right to that position; humanly speaking, we retain it only so long as we are able to retain it by the law of cheapness. No two petty shopkeepers in a country village are more thoroughly competitive in their mutual relations than, for example, England and the United States. Our goods are purchased only while they can be obtained more cheaply here than elsewhere, and our workshops would soon be all silent if the palm of cheapness passed into other hands. The comparative impunity with which we have borne the disastrous effects of strikes demonstrates the strength and elasticity of British resources. We see here how impregnable our commercial position may continue if we do not abandon it in sheer madness. With labour cheap, and yet constantly becoming more skilled in consequence of the spread of education, we may hope that, with wise commercial regulations and the blessing of Divine Providence, our commercial advantages will be long continued.

Facilities of cheap and rapid intercourse are an important auxiliary to the growth of capital. The goods of a manufacturer, except the very small portion he may retain for his own use, are only valuable as they can find a market, and the expense of sending them there must be reckoned into the cost of production. *Cartage* forms a familiar item of expense in building operations, and every farmer reckons that the virtual price of manure depends upon the distance he may have to send for it. In some countries the want of roads presents insuperable barriers to commerce. The interior of Mexico, for instance, abounds in vegetable produce which would find a ready sale for exportation if it could only be brought down to the coast; but such are the difficulties in the way of inland communication, that the price of wheat is often found to be doubled within the compass of a few miles. The principal obstacle to the cultivation of cotton in India is the want of cheap and easy modes of conveyance. In bringing it over the vast plains of Hindostan so large an addition would be made to its original cost, as to leave no chances of its competing successfully with that which we import from the United States. The immense sums invested in highways, canals, and railroads, present in a very striking light the expensiveness of carriage. At the close of 1850 there were six thousand three hundred miles of railway in operation within this country, which had been executed at an average cost of £40,000 per mile, involving a total expenditure of £250,000,000. The railway receipts for the year 1851 amounted to £15,000,000 sterling, a great part of which was spent in merely changing the localities of things, without adding anything to their intrinsic value. We see here the immense advantage of cheap intercourse. An arrangement which would diminish the expense of carriage one-half, would add from one source alone between seven and eight millions annually to the national wealth. But speed is as important an element in locomotion as cheapness ; or rather, a slow process cannot be cheap. While goods are in the act of transfer they are dead to commerce; they are of no use to the buyer, the seller, or any one else. It would be deemed a great sacrifice to lend a person £50,000 for three months without interest, yet goods in passing from place to place resemble money thus lent. Every tradesman knows the value of "quick returns." £400, if it can be turned over three times in the course of twelve months, will be more profitable than £1,000 which returns to the coffers of its owner only once in that period. The invention of railways, by shortening the time of transit, tends to promote quick returns. A merchant who orders goods of the manufacturer may now receive them, sell them again, and make another purchase with the money obtained in exchange in less time than would formerly have elapsed before their delivery.

4. Let us now glance at the relation which exists between capital and the remuneration of labour. This is an important aspect of the subject, and one which borrows peculiar interest from the circumstances of the present time. When the workman is told that cheap

labour is essential to the accumulation of capital, he is apt to ask indignantly, Whether labour is to be bound hand and foot in order to be offered as a victim at the shrine of capital? Whether the poor man is to toil for a mere pittance in order to make a rich man richer? Such bitter recrimination is altogether groundless; it is the fruit of a misunderstanding. The interests of capital and labour are not antagonistic; it is not necessary to offer the one as a holocaust to the other. The cheapest labour which can be wanted is labour at its natural price, and a higher price than this cannot be asked without damaging the interests of the employer, and through him the workman. It is difficult to say whether a proceeding which fetters capital, and thus renders it less accumulative, is more injurious to the master or the workman, since it tends to destroy that without which wages of any amount are impossible.

The accumulation of capital tends directly and necessarily to raise the rate of wages, understanding by that term the command of the conveniences of life which a man receives in return for his labour. Sometimes a higher pecuniary equivalent may be obtained in some branches of labour during the infancy of capital, before the principle of competition has come fairly into play; but competition, in proportion as it lowers the nominal rate of wages, increases their exchangeable value by lowering the price of commodities. Rapidly accumulating capital must evidently have the double effect of increasing the demand for labour, and sharpening the struggle for cheapness. If the profits of the past year enabled one thousand employers each to put £5,000 into his business, they would instantly want more men, since £5,000,000 more money would have to be expended in the erection of workshops, the purchase of materials, and the payment of labour. If they found a sufficient number of persons to suit their purpose already unemployed, there would be so many less to compete with those who are in employment; but if all were already employed they would have to attract workmen by giving higher wages. Thus every addition which is made to the capital of the country tends directly either to keep wages from sinking, or to raise them higher. But such an augmentation of capital reacts upon the real remuneration of labour in another way. A thousand manufacturers, each employing more money and more hands, will produce a greater quantity of goods, and this increased production, unless the demand increase in the same ratio, must render them cheaper. No doubt competition acts on wages too, by forcing the employer to economize in every direction, but its tendency to depress wages is trivial compared with its cheapening power. There is a limit below which the price of labour cannot sink, but no limit has yet been found to the cheapness of production. By improvements in agriculture, mechanical inventions, and an extended market, we know not what luxuries may be brought within the reach of the working man. In this respect a vast change has taken place within the present century. Is not the home of the industrious and *provident* artisan, in many cases, a palace compared with what it would have been fifty years ago? Deal has given way to mahogany; he treads on carpets instead of sand. When weary he reclines on a sofa, or throws himself, it may be, in his spring-bottomed arm-chair. His own dress is of superfine broad cloth, and his wife regards silk as no special luxury. If he is a reading man, every month brings him a packet of magazines; and perhaps at times he recreates his family by the sea-side. Such things could not have been done formerly; they are the direct result of capital and competition, the share which has accrued to labour from the increase which has taken place in the national wealth.

The action of capital as one of the factors concerned in the production of wealth, depends very little upon its being distributed among various hands, or gathered within few. It matters nothing to the man who has his labour to sell, whether a hundred thousand pounds is owned by one individual, or by ten; there it is, to be made profitable by a remunerative investment of some kind; this is the essential fact with which he has to do. As far as the labourer is concerned, the only question which need be asked is, what arrangements will best promote the accumulation of capital, and thus increase the demand for labour? It will even be found, perhaps, that the interests of the operative classes are more advanced by a few large capitalists than by many small ones, since in extensive concerns the business is more economically carried on, and a proportionately smaller sum is required to maintain the establishment, leaving more to be employed in the remuneration of productive labour. The working man is apt to look with a jealous eye upon a person of extensive wealth. He sympathizes with the humble capitalist who is struggling through many difficulties towards a more affluent position; but in proportion as this struggle, so kindly regarded, becomes successful, his sympathetic feelings are changed into those of envy and dread. This, however, is an erroneous condition of matters. The wealthiest man in the state, even if he does not perform a single act of pure benevolence, provided only that he does not squander his money in luxury, but *expends it so as to bring in the largest revenue*, is necessarily, not in spite of his wealth, but by virtue of it, a most useful man.* If his fortune were divided among a thousand persons it would probably be less advantageous to society. Each, feeling himself raised to a higher position, would expend more in personal display, so that, on the whole, considerably fewer workmen would be employed, and at the year's end a considerably smaller addition would be made

* Of course we employ the term useful in a restricted sense.

to the stock of public wealth. On such an arrangement, a thousand persons would be richer, but the aggregate of society would be poorer; a thousand persons would rise from the class of operatives to that of employers, but probably double that number would be thrown altogether out of employ. The centralization of wealth does not, assuming that it is not hoarded by its owner, tend to divide society between the two extremes of affluence and poverty; it merely strengthens, to use a different figure, the advanced guard of society, so that the ranks behind may advance with greater ease and safety. Capital cannot accumulate without tending to make all richer, and whatever arrangement is most favourable to accumulation, is that which must prove most beneficial. Recent tables show that there is in this country an increase in the number of moderate incomes, and a comparative diminution in the number of colossal incomes.

5. No truth within the limits of social science is more demonstrable than that the growth of capital tends to promote the welfare of all classes. When each individual is doing the best he can for himself, the entire community must also be prospering. We see here another illustration of the simplicity which reigns throughout the social structure. The ladder by which mankind ascend from the depths of penury to competence and happiness, is so delicate, so framed in harmony with the very texture of our nature, that it must evidently

be the work of God. Capital spontaneously directs itself into the most lucrative channels. Like a mule upon the mountains, when left to choose its own path it seldom goes wrong, but when coerced by the rider it is danger of plunging down some fatal precipice. Every individual seeks to better his circumstances; the small shopkeeper is always contriving fresh means of turning his money to advantage, he fixes himself in the best situation he can discover, endeavours to win custom, deals in those articles which yield the highest profit, and would at any moment throw the whole business aside if he felt assured that another would prove more lucrative.* If we ascend a few steps higher we find the same principles at work, and so also among the first merchants, bankers, and capitalists of the land. The great manufacturing and agricultural interests of the kingdom are self-adjusted by the same laws. Every person follows his present pursuit till he finds it less remunerative than another, which he instantly chooses in its stead. Thus, of its own accord, the public capital always seeks the most profitable investment; pointing necessarily towards it as the needle to the pole. If a wise king, seeing beforehand the necessity for such an investment of capital, but ignorant of the means which Providence has set apart to secure

* In this and similar places men are spoken of in general terms, or as acting universally according to certain general principles, without taking into account the modifying influences in character and practice arising from religious considerations.

it, were resolved to accomplish the same object by legislation, what a herculean task would he impose upon himself! what innumerable laws would have to be enacted! what a multitude of details would have to be kept in view! what a host of functionaries would have to be constantly employed! It would be necessary to put every capitalist in the land under strict surveillance, to examine all his schemes, and forbid the investment of a farthing till its probable value had been gauged by authorized intellect. How slow and agonizing would be the progress of society on such a system; or rather, checked on every hand, held in such a state of unnatural tension from all quarters, how soon would it break in pieces! God has legislated on this question, and in his own manner. The voice which said, "Let there be light," has spoken here in language equally simple. Each person, in providing for his own welfare, provides to a certain extent also for the welfare of the whole. The Divine arrangement is, let each person, charitable and just in all his dealings, employ what he has in that way which seems likeliest to him to produce more. To oppose this regulation in any way is only selfish in a state of ignorance, since it is the only one which harmonizes with the progress and well-being of society.

When this regulation is strictly observed, its beneficial results are innumerable. Since no pursuit can be more remunerative than another without attracting capital, and occasioning increased production and competition within itself, it insures the proper distribution of capital among the various branches of trade, and guarantees the public that every article shall be furnished them at the lowest possible cost. It stimulates and rewards industry, suffers no man to vegetate with impunity, withers the unwatered vineyard, and increases with substance the diligent hand. It exacts intelligence as one of the chief aids to social development; the possession of knowledge sufficient to enable each person to choose those departments of labour which are most profitable, and to acquiesce in the utility of the general system. This is one of the chief wants of society at the present time. The popular dissatisfaction which is levelled against capital can be dissipated only by the schoolmaster. Not one educated person in a thousand inveighs against capital; our Owens and Proudhoms are rare. But an incomparably larger portion of the uneducated classes do so, and the only way to diminish it is to enlighten them. Yes, it is a trace of the finger of an almighty Architect, that capital is necessitated in its own defence to educate the people. But even knowledge is not the highest requisite to the increase of capital—the virtues are still more necessary. Prudence, industry, sobriety, honesty, perseverance, benevolence, gratitude; and if these, then also those Divine principles which are most favourable to their production, are indispensable to the maintenance of that vigorous social life which God has made the absolute condition of social progress.

It will be interesting, after this brief view of the nature and tendencies of capital, to glance at some of its effects. Fully to present all these in their proper magnitude would involve a history of our social progress during the last fifty years; but a few facts, selected chiefly from the admirable work on this subject by the late Mr. R. G. Porter, will suffice for the end we have in view. Let us first glance at the probable amount of our present accumulations—the fund out of which our future enterprises must be carried on. One of the great divisions under which the national capital distributes itself is that of personal property. A moment's reflection will show us that it is impossible to ascertain the amount of this with absolute accuracy; still we are able, from the produce of the legacy duty which falls upon that description of wealth, to form an approximate estimate. Before giving the result of Mr. Porter's calculations, it will be useful to understand the method by which it is obtained. It is found that the proportion of deaths annually among the heads of families, or those who leave property, is about one in forty-five. Out of every ten who die, not more than three leave property of sufficient importance to require a will. The aggregate value of the effects belonging to the remaining seven must be far from inconsiderable, but still as we have no means of ascertaining its amount, and as it must be comparatively small, we may leave it out of view, and consider the personality of the three wealthy individuals as the amount bequeathed by the whole. Thus the capital which pays the legacy duty in any one year may be regarded as having belonged to all the persons who die within the same, and to bear a similar proportion to the entire personal property within the realm, as those persons bear to the entire population. But the latter proportion is found to be, as we have stated, about one in forty-five, and therefore the capital charged with legacy duty in the year may be regarded as one-forty-fifth of the aggregate amount of the same species of wealth in the hands of the community. On such data, Mr. Porter estimates the value of personal property held within this realm in 1841 at £2,000,000,000. This immense amount has been reached by progressive steps. In 1797, the capital charged with legacy duty amounted in round numbers to a million sterling, whilst during the next four decades it advanced respectively to nine, thirty-three, thirty-four, and forty-two millions. We may judge by this test how rapidly we grew in wealth during the period referred to, an addition of eight hundred millions having been added to our stock of capital in the twenty-four years preceding 1841. If we turn to that species of property which consists in land, houses, mines, etc., we meet with an amount equally startling. Sir Robert Peel, in introducing his proposal for an income-tax in 1842, assumed the annual value of real property at £72,800,000, which sum at twenty-five years' purchase is equal to a capital of £1,820,000,000. The advance which has taken place in the amount of real property since 1815 is strikingly illustrated in the case of Manchester and Salford. In the former of these boroughs the total increase from that period till 1841 was no less than £16,716,975, or 189 per cent., while in Salford the increase was still greater, being as much as 194 per cent.

The impression made by figures when they relate to such vast sums is necessarily rather vague, and a more definite idea may be obtained by looking at a few of those enterprises on which our wealth has been expended. We have already mentioned railways, and the expenditure of two hundred and fifty millions employed in their construction. This is a monument of affluence which has not been erected without peril; there are thousands, unhappily, who will never forget the panic which occurred a few years ago, in consequence of a sudden and disproportionate investment of money in railway schemes; but still, the fact that such a vast amount has been permanently sunk in merely providing us with better facilities of locomotion, affords pleasing evidence of the extent of our resources. During the first forty years of the present century, 4,400,000 tons of shipping were built and registered within the United Kingdom. Assuming that the work was executed at an average cost of £30 a ton, we have here an outlay of £132,000,000. Probably £7,000,000 were expended during the same period in the construction of new roads, while the annual expenditure of the various turnpike trusts in England and Wales amounted in 1840 to more than a million and a half. The capital sunk in canals is about £11,000,000 sterling. It is surprising what vast sums have been laid out in the improvement of towns and the erection of public buildings. The corporation of Liverpool, in the course of fifty years, expended £1,600,000 on this object; and a single improvement in Newcastle-on-Tyne was effected at the cost of £2,000,000. Since the beginning of the century, London has spent £8,000,000 in the construction of docks, and £4,000,000 in bridges. If we estimate the places set apart for the purpose of public worship throughout the country at 25,000, and allow to each an average value of £2,000, we find here an additional item of £50,000,000. Vast sums have been spent in supplying our large towns with water. The corporation of Manchester are at present engaged in an undertaking of this kind at an outlay of £650,000. The agricultural productiveness of the country is probably twice as great now as it was at the beginning of the century; and this is all due to the application of a greater amount of capital to the soil. But the most impressive illustration of British wealth is to be found in the growth of our foreign trade. "The amount of tonnage employed in the conveyance of products to and from our shores, forms a much better measure of the progress of our foreign trade than any computation of their cost in money. If, then, we contrast the amount of shipping which entered and left our ports in the two years, (1802 and 1836,) we find that in the former year it amounted to less than half the tonnage employed in the latter." The population of Great Britain is now nearly double what it was towards the close of the last century, and yet it may be safely asserted that all classes live in a state of much greater comfort now than at any former period. Work is not less abundant, the rate of wages is little if at all lowered, while a very great and general reduction has taken place in the price of commodities. What supports the nine or ten millions which have been added to the population? To furnish them gratuitously with the means of subsistence would be a gigantic act of pauperism, sufficient to bankrupt the richest state; but capital, leaguing itself with labour, not only maintains them in a high condition of comfort, but lays by a surplus which, in the course of a few years, will suffice for the maintenance of millions more. It heightens our impression of the astonishing capabilities of trade to reflect that our present position has been reached in the face of an enormous public expenditure; the money required to carry on the war with Napoleon having amounted in one year (1814) to £100,000,000; and our wars have laden us with a permanent debt to nearly eight times that amount. If, in spite of such obstacles, we have realized so much prosperity, what would have been the result of uninterrupted peace? We cannot hesitate to admit that if those vast sums had been employed in remunerative industry, "an amount of prosperity would have been experienced that must have had the happiest effects upon the physical and moral condition of England first, and through England upon the whole European family."

In the present day, proof is abundant on all hands that not only is capital increasing, but that its legitimate fruits have been largely produced in the augmented well-being of all classes.* The declared value of our exports in 1840 was, in round numbers, fifty millions; in 1845 it amounted to sixty millions; while in 1850 it reached seventy-four millions. The returns of 1851 show an increase, as compared with 1848, of twenty-one millions. While we have exported more for the use of other nations, we have also imported considerably more of their surplus commodities for our own. The rapid growth of our imports within the last few years is without a parallel. In 1840 they amounted to sixty-seven millions, in 1845 to eighty-five millions, and in 1850 to one hundred millions. Notwithstanding the largeness of our exports, a larger proportion of cotton

* See the speech of the Chancellor of the Exchequer on opening the Budget, 1852.

manufactures was retained for home consumption during 1851 than during any previous year. Since 1831, taxes to the amount of nineteen millions have been abolished. Twenty years ago the sum appropriated to the relief of the poor was nearly ten shillings per head of the whole population; in 1851 it was little more than five shillings and sixpence. At that period the number of depositors in savings' banks was only 412,217, and the sum deposited £13,507,565; in 1851 the number of depositors was 1,161,838, and the sum deposited had risen to £30,184,604, being an advance from twelve shillings and eightpence to one pound two shillings and threepence per head of the whole population. The increase of social intercourse may be inferred from the fact that in 1831 the newspaper stamps issued from the Stamp Office were twenty millions, and in 1851 had risen to eighty millions; and while the number of letters posted in the former year was sixty millions, in the latter it reached three hundred and forty-seven millions sixty-nine thousand. Thirty years ago, the whole of our wool imports were but nine millions seven hundred thousand pounds; in 1851 they were eighty-one millions. In exact accordance with the tendencies of increasing capital, as explained in this chapter, prices have fallen from twenty to forty per cent., while wages have scarcely declined, and in some instances have greatly advanced. In Birmingham, in 1851, 1,329 new houses were built, almost double the number of any preceding year, and almost entirely by the smaller class of tradespeople. In the same place pauperism has declined four-fifths, while artizans alone have invested £70,000 in freehold land societies. Similar facts might be recorded of other towns. In pauper maintenance there has been a diminution of eleven per cent. throughout the country in the latter half of 1851 as compared with 1850. The creation of mills, factories, docks, wharfs, and warehouses goes on apace. Since 1848, our mercantile shipping has increased by two hundred and fifty thousand tons, and taken into employ three thousand additional men. These are cheering facts. We have cause, it is true, in many respects, for national humiliation, especially in the insane and wicked excesses of a speculating mania, which subjects us to a periodical panic, and in the condition of our sister island. Still even here cheering signs of improvement are visible. The unforgotten calamities which happened six years ago are teaching us to unite wisdom and moderation with commercial enterprise, and prefer safe profits to brilliant but hazardous measures; while the social and religious movements now going on in Ireland are full of happy auguries for the future, as Popery apparently is losing its ascendency over the popular mind. In these and other causes of the present day we discern, we trust, a renewing of our youth; the beginning, not the end of our career. We have only, under God's blessing, to proceed with intelligence and firmness in order to place our prosperity on an infrangible basis. Nothing can ruin, no earthly power can subdue, a patriotic and industrious people, whose institutions are based on justice, and pervaded by a spirit of true religion. Such, we trust, is our true prospect. Every lover of his country must rejoice at it, while the Christian citizen will "thank God, and take courage."

CHAPTER IV.

MONEY CURRENT: A FEW WORDS ABOUT GOLD, SILVER, AND BANK NOTES

Gold and silver are the most remarkable constituents of wealth. They are so not only because they have a greater value in proportion to their bulk than most other commodities, but because the value of all other commodities is referred to them as its measure and symbol. If we want to ascertain the wealth of a person, we ask, How much money is he worth? If he is anxious to grow rich, we say he is eager to make money. A thousand other articles may be refused as part of a bargain, but no one thinks of refusing money. Gold and silver resemble the hero of romance, at whose approach the strongest bolts fly back, and the heaviest doors swing open.

Let us briefly consider the nature and origin of money. We have mentioned the division of labour as one of the sources of wealth. This principle, when once thoroughly adopted, not only tends to increase the aggregate riches of the community, but to change the whole aspect of its affairs. At first each man worked for himself, supplying his wants as best he could without the help of his neighbour. This phase of society, if it was ever anything more than theoretic, soon vanished. Mankind found it mutually advantageous to work for each other. Instead of bewildering themselves with a Babel of conflicting occupations, the farmer kept to his plough, the smith to his forge, and the cobbler to his last. But here a new process commenced. Of the numerous wants the farmer experienced, his home-grown wheat would supply only one. He would therefore have to divide the remainder of his wheat into so many lots, and carry them where they could be exchanged for other commodities. This process was a new era in civilization—it inaugurated the principle of exchange.

But the process did not stop here; it soon led to another phenomenon. The function of exchanging was soon assigned to one commodity in preference to others, and this commodity was called *money*. The convenience of this change would soon be found very great. The farmer now, instead of dividing his wheat into as many different lots as he had wants to provide for, might, if he so chose, sell all the produce of his farm to one person, who would pay him for it in gold or silver, with which he might at any moment purchase the articles he might require. He would thus obtain an imperishable article in the place of a perishable one. Should he, owing to a favourable season, obtain more wheat than was requisite to meet his immediate wants, he would be able to turn it into something which damp could not spoil, nor mice devour. Moreover, he would be able to use money with more facility than the produce of his farm. He could carry two pieces of gold or silver to the smith, or the tailor, much more easily than a sack of corn. Agricultural produce, it is true, being generally capable of minute subdivision, might be used in purchasing small quantities of other commodities, but all would not be equally successful with the farmer in this respect. The grazier, for example, whose property consisted of so many head of oxen, would often be unable, if confined to the method of barter, to purchase the exact quantity of salt or flour which he might have occasion for. He would evidently be obliged to buy as much as would be an equivalent for a single ox, or some multiple of that value; he could not buy a quantity equal in value to half an ox, or an ox and a half. But the adoption of money as an instrument of exchange would put all such inconveniences aside. The grazier might sell his oxen, and with the proceeds purchase any amount of whatever he might require. For these and similar reasons money must soon have come into general use. So early as the time of Abraham, it was the common medium of exchange. The silver which he weighed to the children of Heth for the field and cave of Machpelah, was "current money with the merchants."

Some writers have thrown considerable

mystery round the origin cf money. It has been regarded by some as the peculiar instrument of taxation; a mere device of kingly tyranny. This view conceals its true nature. Instead of being forced into circulation as an arbitrary equivalent for commodities which had been forcibly seized in the name of the sovereign, it was adopted on account of its intrinsic utility. Money in all ages has been, not a mere symbol of value, but a real valuable. Whatever may have been used for that purpose, whether the precious metal or any other costly article, it never purchased more than it appeared to be *worth.* A bank note would cease to circulate as money if it did not bind the party issuing it to pay the bearer the sum specified thereon. A thousand pounds not only measures the value for a certain quantity of goods, but has itself an equal and independent value of its own. The silver which Abraham paid in exchange for Sarah's burial-place, though he could neither eat nor drink it, was as truly a part of his wealth as his sheep and cattle. The tastes of mankind have always risen higher than the mere satisfying their bodily wants. They have aimed, not merely at living, but at living in elegance and splendour. Hence, silver and gold, being appropriate to the purposes of decoration, constituted as true an element of wealth as food itself.

As the use of money is simply the exchanging of one commodity for another, convenience alone determined that silver and gold should become the common medium of exchange. The choice of these metals for such a purpose was not made, however, without good reasons. Some of these are evident. Scarcely any other article is less liable to decay. A bar of gold will sustain little injury in the course of a thousand years. They are also both hard and fusible, easily divided into any number of parts to suit the convenience of the dealer, and nearly unite the maximum of value with the minimum of bulk. The most important characteristic of the precious metals is, that they are so scarce, and the labour required to procure them is so great, as to secure us from any considerable or sudden alteration in their value. This is a fundamental point. If a person, in concluding some purchase, agreed to pay another in twelve months' time six quarters of wheat, there would be a danger of his creditor obtaining more or less than his due, since the accident of a good or bad harvest next autumn might raise or sink the price of that article by one-half, and affect in such a ratio the terms of the bargain. But it is impossible that the quantity of gold in circulation next year should differ so far from its present amount. During that short interval its variation in price will be very inconsiderable, and hence a payment fixed in it will fluctuate in value much less than if it were fixed in corn. But though this is true in reference to comparatively short intervals, a different law holds good when we speak of centuries: A quarter of wheat is much more likely to retain the same value in relation to other commodities at the beginning and the end of an era of three hundred years than a sum of money. Of this, Dr. Adam Smith mentions a remarkable instance. "By the eighteenth of Elizabeth, it was enacted that a third of the rent of all college leases should be reserved in corn, to be paid either in kind, or according to the current prices at the nearest market. The money arising from the corn rent, though originally but a third of the whole, is, in the present times, according to Dr. Blackstone, commonly nearly double of what arises from the other two-thirds. The old money rents of colleges must, according to this account, have sunk to almost a fourth of their ancient value, or are worth little more than a fourth of the corn they were originally worth. Some ancient rents in Scotland, originally of considerable value, have in this manner been reduced almost to nothing." All payments, therefore, which are intended to be made for centuries to come at a uniform value should not be fixed in money. The same quantities of corn will, at distant times, be much nearer the same value in relation to other commodities than the same quantities of gold or silver.

It is common to speak of barter as a transaction essentially different from one which is effected by means of money, the name being applied to an exchange of commodities of one sort for those of another, as distinct from an exchange of commodities for coin. Such a distinction may be useful, but it has no real basis. The precious metals are as truly commodities as sugar and cotton. A purchase is not essentially different from simple barter, and whatever we give in exchange for some other article is money. Because the merchant finds it more convenient both to the seller and himself to effect the purchase by giving the precious metals rather than timber, salt, or flax, the nature of the process is not at all altered. It was not mere accident which determined that gold and silver should be used as money. If these metals had been less durable or of less value in proportion to their bulk, some other articles would have been adopted in their stead. In very ancient times the Greek or Roman merchant drove his oxen to the smith's shop to obtain in exchange the productions of the forge; but when, observing that a piece of gold of a certain size and quality was regarded as equal in value to so many oxen, he preferred using it in his commerce with the smith: no mystery was thrown around the process; he merely chose, from motives of private convenience, to part with one kind of property rather than another.

It is amusing to observe how many different kinds of articles have been actually used for money. There is evidence that sheep and oxen were extensively employed for this purpose in the earliest ages. The illustration usually drawn from Homer, that the armour of Diomede cost nine oxen, while that of Glaucus cost a hundred, will probably be familiar to the readei. Hence the first coined money is supposed to have borne an impress of the animal whose value it represented. An instance of this occurs in Job xlii. 11, where it is said, that every one of Job's friends "gàve him a piece of *money*." The term used in the original is *kesitoth*, thought by some to denote a sheep or a lamb, but the most correct translation may be presumed to be that which favours the idea of a piece of money bearing a stamp indicating that it was of the value of a sheep or lamb. The generic name for money among the Romans, *pecunia*, points to the same origin, having been derived from *pecus*, signifying *cattle*. In some parts of Africa, pieces of cloth, of a certain size and quality, constitute, so to speak, the current coin. In other parts of the same continent, cowry shells serve for money, and elsewhere cakes of salt. In some parts of the East Indies, fine porcelain shells answer the same purpose; and among some of the American tribes, wampum, or strings of shells, which may be worn round the waist, serve both for ornaments and money. Among the same people, as also among the ancient Russians, and all primitive nations, skins were a common medium of exchange. This fact elucidates that passage in Job where the patriarch says, "Skin for skin, (literally, skin after skin,) yea, all that a man hath will he give for his life," pointing to the universal truth that the love of existence is so strong within the human breast, that men are willing to purchase it, though at the cost of all their earthly provisions.

Gold and silver, which now constitute the principal medium of exchange among civilized nations, have been found in abundance in many different parts of the globe from the earliest times. The first accounts we have of these precious metals are found in the Scriptures. The sacred historian, speaking of the river Pison, probably the Euphrates, says, "It compasseth the whole land of Havilah, where there is gold, and the gold of that land is good." Abraham is said to have been rich "in cattle, in silver, and in gold;" and Job beautifully exclaims, at the opening of the sublime passage in which he delineates the nature and excellence of true wisdom: "Surely there is a vein for the silver, and a place for the gold where they fine it." The comparative abundance of gold at a little later period is proved by the large supply which the children of Israel carried with them out of Egypt. The tabernacle erected out of their voluntary offerings was a costly structure; its walls and a great part of its furniture were overlaid with gold. The entire value of the precious metals employed in its construction is estimated by Dr. Kitto at £213,320. Taking into account the social condition of the children of Israel in Egypt, and making proper allowances for the valuable gifts which they received from the Egyptians at their departure, we cannot but conclude that in those early days gold was very plentiful in proportion to the population.* We learn again from the sacred records, that in the time of Solomon gold abounded in Palestine. The reign of Solomon may be regarded as an epoch in the history of that metal. He collected in one year six hundred threescore and ten talents, probably about £300,000 in value of our money, and his ships brought from Ophir 420 talents of gold, or £190,800. We are told in the book of Kings that his throne was of ivory overlaid with gold, that all the drinking vessels were of gold, and all the vessels of the house of the forest of Lebanon were of pure gold; none were of silver, for silver was "nothing accounted of in the days of Solomon," who "made silver to be as stones in Jerusalem." He also made "two hundred targets of beaten gold; six hundred shekels of gold went to one target: and three hundred shields of beaten gold; three pounds of gold went to one shield."

These statements of the inspired volume, from which we should infer the comparative abundance of gold among the nations of antiquity, are strikingly confirmed by profane history.† Diodorus informs us that Ninus, the founder of Nineveh, "possessed himself of all the treasures of Bactriana, among which was abundance of silver and gold;" and that "Semiramis, the founder of Babylon, erected statues

* The Tabernacle and its Furniture, by Dr. Kitto.

† For many of the facts embodied in this chapter the author is indebted to the valuable "Lectures on Gold," which have recently been delivered at the Museum of Practical Geology.

of beaten gold, that of Jupiter being forty feet in height, and weighing a thousand Babylonian talents, and those of Rhea and Juno equalling it in size and magnificence." From the accounts given by Diodorus, it is inferred that Semiramis had collected as much gold as would amount to eleven millions of our money. The tribute which Darius king of Persia drew from his various provinces amounted in gold alone, according to the calculations of Gibbon, to £3,250,000. We may jud , of the proverbial wealth of Crœsus, king of Lydia, who lived 540 years before Christ, by the value of his presents to the temple of Delphi, which amounted to 4,000 talents of silver, and 270 talents of gold, a sum nearly equal to £3,500,000 sterling. The enormous wealth of Pytheus, a Lydian despot of the age of Xerxes, enabled him to entertain that monarch with his whole army, when on their way to invade Greece. He even offered to defray the whole expense of the expedition, a piece of generosity which Xerxes ill repaid by putting his son to death, rather than suffer him, at his father's request, to leave the army. The metallic treasures of Pytheus have been estimated at £3,600,000 of our money. Appian tells us that in the time of Ptolemy Philadelphus the Egyptian treasury contained no less a sum than £178,000,000. The immense wealth of the Romans may be inferred from the following facts. The sums obtained by Augustus through the testamentary bequests of his friends amounted to £32,291,666 sterling. Tiberius left at his death a fortune of £21,796,875, which Caligula is said to have squandered in a single year. The sum required for the maintenance of the Roman commonwealth was estimated, at the accession of Vespasian, at £322,916,000 sterling. Cæsar, before setting out for Spain, is said to have been £2,018,000 in debt, and two of the bribes which he lavished for the maintenance of his political power were together more than three quarters of a million sterling.

It would be interesting to inquire into the source from which the ancients drew these immense supplies of the precious metals, but the intricacy of the subject precludes us from venturing more than a few general remarks, in which we shall still avail ourselves of the guidance of Mr. Hunt. Humboldt thinks it probable that large quantities were brought by the Phœnicians from western India and the adjacent coasts of Arabia and eastern Africa. It is probable that gold was found in abundance in the countries bordering on the north-eastern corner of the Black Sea. Here, Herodotus tell us, the Massagetæ had accumulated an immense quantity of gold, and here too the Siberian gold washings have been found so lucrative that whereas they yielded but £8,345 in the year 1830, their value increased more than a hundred fold during the next twelve years, and are now the source of a considerable revenue to the Russian government. Very extensive gold-works, evidently abandoned for many centuries past, have been discovered on the south-eastern slope of the Ural Mountains. They were worked, in all probability, by the Scythian tribes to whom Herodotus refers. "Their extent shows that the workmen employed in them must have been numerous, while an inspection of them proves that only the rudiments of the science of mining were then known. They seem to have scraped out the gold with boars' fangs, and collected it in leather bags or packets. Some of the pits are twenty fathoms deep. The roots of large fir-trees have spread themselves among the heaps of stones which have been raised against the sides of the furnaces." Gold was also procured in large quantities from Ethiopia and Nubia. Belzoni discovered that an extensive tract had been worked in the Sahara Mountains, and Jacobs infers, from a close examination of the subject, that the produce of these mines was not less than £6,000,000 annually, a large proportion of which must have been gold. Hence probably the Pharaohs drew their wealth. Here, perhaps, the gold was produced which was consecrated to the service of God in the Jewish Tabernacle, and that which along with costly spices, constituted the valuable presents which the queen of Sheba offered to king Solomon. The Athenians procured gold from Thrace and the isle of Thasos; Thessaly also produced ores which were rich in the same metal. The Romans drew their enormous wealth from various sources; from Upper Italy and Spain; the Novi Alps and Illyria. From this last district gold was obtained, partly in large grains on the surface, and partly in mines, in so fine a state that only an eighth part was lost in the process of smelting and refining. Its great quantity caused a decrease of its price by one-third throughout Italy, and induced the proprietors to employ fewer workmen in order to raise its value. We have seen that the wealth of Rome during the Augustan age was immense, but it soon declined very rapidly in consequence of the closing of the mines in Illyria and Spain, and for a long period the world received no addition to its stock of the precious metals.

Coming down to more modern times, it is interesting to notice the traces of gold which have been found on our own soil. It is probable that the Romans were led to invade Britain in consequence of the reports they had heard of its excessive wealth. It is certain that they worked the Gogofau mines in Caermarthenshire. Small quantities of gold have also been picked up in Cornwall from the earliest times, and in the reigns of Edward I. and III., extensive works were carried on at Comb Martin, Devonshire; between 300 and 400 miners from Derbyshire were employed in them, and their produce was so considerable as to assist the Black Prince in his wars against France. In 1390, Richard II. granted to John Younge, refiner, all the gold and silver found in any mine in England, on condition of his paying a ninth part to the crown, a tenth to the church, and an eleventh to the proprietor of the soil. Such was the rage for gold in the middle ages, that it became one of the leading objects of philosophic pursuit. In 1444, a patent was granted to John Cobbe, "that by the art of philosophy he might transform imperfect metals from their own proper nature, and transmute them to gold or silver." In the eighth century, the Hungarian gold mines were first worked, and in the following century those of Sweden and Norway; but during the next five hundred years, the quantity of gold produced from mines was probably not more than sufficient to make up for the annual waste of that already in circulation. The discovery of America in 1492 was soon followed by considerable accession of metallic wealth, though on the whole, the general impression which prevails respecting its amount is probably exaggerated. The extravagant expectations of Columbus and his companions were greatly disappointed. The Indians were strangers to the arts of mining, and the little gold they had in their possession had been picked up on the surface of the earth, or found in the channels of their mountain streams. The Spaniards, however, soon began to search for the precious metals with the appliances of European skill; extensive works were set on foot; still, to 1519, the annual yield of gold was not more than £52,000. Pizarro landed in Peru in 1527, and during the next twenty-five years America forwarded to Spain, according to the calculation of Humboldt, £630,000 per annum in gold, which would make the total produce of gold in America from 1492 to 1545, a period of fifty-three years, about £17,058,000 sterling, or a little more than £321,849 annually. In 1545, the celebrated silver mines of Potosi were discovered, the annual produce of which for the next twenty-one years was equal in value to £280,000 sterling.

It is impossible to think of the sufferings inflicted upon the American aborigines, in this merciless struggle for gain, without pity. The unhappy native soon found that the possession of gold was equivalent to a sentence of proscription and massacre. The excesses of the ruthless hordes which followed the banners of Cortes and Pizarro to the New World will ever stand among the most cruel and loathsome tragedies which pollute the historic page. They demonstrate to the world that mammon is as bloodthirsty as ambition, and that the happiness, and the lives of millions are sometimes as cheap at the shrine of money as at the shrine of power. When the natives had yielded to their invaders all the precious metals in their possession, they were straightway reduced to slavery, and forced to ransack the earth for more. Hard labour, prosecuted under the lash of their cruel taskmasters, destroyed those whom the sword had spared; and if the severities at first resorted to had long continued, extinction would soon have covered with its shroud the hapless race of Montezuma. Avarice at length supplied its own correction, and the fear of having no slaves to toil dictated the exercise of moderation. For three centuries, however, the chief use which Spain made of her enormous colonial empire was that of ministering to domestic luxury. Vast treasures were annually dispatched to the mother country, which contributed to its immediate wealth at the expense of plunging it in irremediable poverty. Had the wealth derived from the colonies been employed in stimulating domestic industry, or been absorbed in the demands of an increasing commerce, it would have proved a source of permanent benefit. But instead of being applied to these objects, it was sought merely as the means of present gratification. Agriculture was neglected, trade discouraged, but little capital expended in home enterprises; the nation strove, as far as possible, to live on the income derived from the precarious source of its transatlantic possessions, and when this was cut off it became at once poor. Thus we see how the colonial wealth which once made Spain an object of envy to other nations, by discouraging productive industry, the only true basis of national greatness, conduced to her present prostration, and thus the selfishness of her councils became in this way the executor of its own deserved punishment.

From 1760 to 1769 the value of the silver produce of the Mexican mines amounted to 112,828,860 dollars. A more liberal policy on the part of the home government raised this during the period 1780–89 to 193,504,554 dollars, and during the next nine years the aggregate produce amounted to 231,080,214 dollars. The disasters of the French revolution, by diminishing the resources of the state, obliged the proprietors of mines to depend for capital upon the advances of private speculators; this led to a narrowing of mining operations, and a consequent diminution of their produce. The severest blow, however, was struck in 1810, when the Mexican revolution forced most of the old Spaniards to withdraw their capital from the country. The condition of the mines in 1823, upon the establishment of the republic, was most deplorable. Nearly all the works had gone to decay, the passages being choked up and the shafts filled with water. The want of domestic capital led to the establishment of foreign companies, by whom the mines were for the most part reclaimed, though at a vast expenditure, and with no prospect of remuneration for years. Many of these enterprises, after exciting hopes of large profits, turned out utter failures. Humboldt calculates that the quantity of silver which the mines of Mexico yielded prior to 1803 amounted to the enormous sum of 1,767,952,000 dollars. Notwithstanding the abstraction of such a vast amount, Mr. Ward declares his conviction that the mineral treasures of New Spain, so far from being exhausted, were scarcely touched; and Humboldt gives it as his opinion that the great mineral resources of Mexico began at precisely that point where the labours of the Spaniards terminated. It serves to correct the impressions likely to be conveyed by such statements to learn that Mexico, though poorly cultivated, possesses in her agriculture a greater source of wealth than all her mines. Humboldt calculates that the agricultural produce of Mexico annually, upon an average of ten years, amounts to twenty-nine millions of dollars. On the other hand, the annual average produce of the Mexican mines amounted, before the revolution of 1810, to twenty-four millions of dollars, being less in value by five millions than the produce of agriculture.*

After a cessation of gold discoveries for more than three centuries, our own times have witnessed a revival of that excitement which the tales of the Spanish navigators formerly spread through Europe. Ever since the termination of the revolutionary war between Great Britain and her North American colonies, a growing importance has been attached to the extensive tract of fertile and unoccupied country which extends from the western side of the Rocky Mountains to the Pacific. It was foreseen that in the spread of civilization westward the time must arrive when that part of the world would become the seat of rising states, but no expectation was entertained that its mineral treasures would soon render its name as synonymous for wealth as that of Peru. Scarcely five years have elapsed since the "diggings" commenced in California, yet the land is already in the

* Ward's Travel's in Mexico.

hands of a rapidly increasing population, towns and villages are springing up in the desert, the various forms of civil society have been extemporized into existence, and its political rights been recognised in the halls of Congress. So early as 1849, nearly 50,000 persons were conveyed across the Isthmus of Panama alone, besides those who chose other routes, on their way to San Francisco, and the ratio of migration has gone on increasing.

While all eyes were turned to California as the world's El Dorado, a golden beam suddenly shone forth from another quarter, which is invested with far superior interest by its political and social connexion with ourselves. Australia, as is well known, is an immense tract of land in the Pacific Ocean, almost as large as all Europe, with the large island called Van Diemen's Land at its south-eastern extremity, and separated from it by Bass Straits about 130 miles across. Emigration to this part of the world had gone on rather slowly. Its distance, the comparatively unattractive nature of its soil, and the bad reputation it had acquired as the seat of our penal settlements, had induced the intending emigrant to choose some other part in preference. In its physical characteristics and the extent of its population, the south-eastern section of this vast continent is the most remarkable. Here are found the most considerable rivers and mountains which have yet been discovered within its limits. The great eastern chain of mountains commences at Wilson's Promontory, opposite

Van Diemen's Land, and stretches north and north-east to the Australian Alps, where it attains, in Mount Kosciusko, an elevation of 6,500 feet. From the Australian Alps, the range continues toward the district of Moreton Bay, at a distance of 70 or 100 miles from the sea, rising occasionally to the height of 4,000 feet. The principal auriferous spots which have yet been discovered occur in the flanks of this mountainous range, or on its lateral spurs and branches. The general character of the gold district will be best understood by approaching it from the neighbourhood of Sydney or Paramatta. Beyond the latter of these towns, which lies the furthest inland, we find for thirty or forty miles a gently undulating plain, only slightly raised above the level of the sea. Beyond this the ground becomes hilly, and slopes gradually upwards for many miles, till it reaches an elevation of perhaps 2,000 feet. The greater part of this sloping surface is intersected with innumerable gullies and ravines, "so that its whole area seems equally divided between the furrows and their separating walls of rock. These gullies have for the most part perfectly precipitous sides, at the bottom of which there is generally a little trickling stream, which after heavy rains is swollen to a fierce torrent. The higher we ascend, the deeper and grander do these ravines become, till they almost assume the character of great gulfs or bays 1,500 feet deep, with grand vertical precipices winding round them in headland after headland, like the Alps of some great seashore. Crossing these mountains, which is a work of no ordinary difficulty, we find ourselves in the Bathurst Plains, a lofty table-land, more than 2,000 feet above the level of the sea. About thirty miles across these plains rises the Conobalas group of hills, attaining a height of 2,300 feet above the level of Bathurst. On the northern flank of these Conobalas several small streams run down into the Macquarrie river, and it was upon the banks of two of these small streams, the Summer Hill Creek and the Lewis Ponds River, that gold was first found. "The gold was found in the accumulated sand and gravel, especially in the inside of the banks of the brook, and at the junction of the two water-courses, where they would often check each other. It was coarse gold, showing its parent site to be no great distance, and probably in the quartz veins traversing the metamorphic rocks of the Conobalas."

The discovery of gold in Australia is peculiarly interesting, because the way to it was opened by scientific thought. Sir Roderick Murchison may be regarded as the true discoverer. That gentleman having visited the Ural Mountains, where gold is found in large quantities, was struck with the resemblance between that district and the great eastern chain of Australia, and so early as 1844, in his address to the Geographical Society, expressed his opinion that the latter would prove auriferous. His remarks having been inserted in the Australian papers, a Mr. Smith, then engaged in some iron works at Berrima, was induced by them to go in search of gold. His search proved successful. He sent his specimens to the colonial government, offering for £500 to reveal the place where they were found. This offer was declined; the governor engaged, however, if Mr. Smith would mention the locality, to reward him according to the value of the discovery. To those terms Mr. Smith refused to accede, and it remained for Mr. Hargraves, who had gained considerable experience in California, to remake the discovery, and obtain the reward from government on their own conditions. The gold was found at first in large quantities. Some of the facts narrated are very remarkable. Mr. Latrobe, lieutenant-governor of Victoria, states that he witnessed the washing of two tins of blue clay, of about twenty-six inches in diameter, and that "the yield" was no less than eight pounds' weight of pure gold. The average produce of the Ballarat diggings was estimated for some time at seven hundred ounces per day. Mount Alexander was still more productive. The gold raised there in December, 1851, was calculated by hundredweights, and brought into the cities on the coast at the rate of two tons a week. The excitement produced throughout the whole colony by such astonishing discoveries can with difficulty be conceived. The towns poured their population into the country. In the district last mentioned 20,000 persons were soon congregated. This sudden absorption of labour in one pursuit, joined to the enormous influx of gold, produced an instantaneous change in the price of every other commodity. Wages in the public departments rose at once fifty or a hundred per cent. Police, turnkeys, letter-carriers, instead of 4*s.* 6*d.* received from 7*s.* to 8*s.* a day. Labourers' wages rose from 5*s.* to 15*s.* and 20*s.* a day, and those of artisans from eighty to a hundred and twenty per cent. The price of food rose in proportion. The quartern loaf, which could formerly be procured for 5*d.*, at the beginning of the present year sold for 1*s.* 3*d.*, and at the last account for 1*s.* 8*d.* The price of meat was doubled, and bacon rose from 6*d.* to 2*s.* a pound. House-rent, hotel charges, cartage, and boat-hire, rose fifty per cent.; clothes, hardware, and furniture, a hundred per cent.; and the price of shoeing a horse, formerly 5*s.*, was now 25*s.* These changes in the price of commodities may be ascribed chiefly to the abandonment of ordinary industrial pursuits, and the sudden increase of the population. During the last six months of 1851, no less than 11,000 persons arrived by sea at the colony of Victoria, and during the first seventeen days of 1852, 2,781.

We have already mentioned the capability which gold has of resisting the influences of the atmosphere as peculiarly fitting it for answering the purpose of money; its extreme malleability renders it equally fit for articles of decoration. It may be beaten into leaves no thicker than $\frac{1}{282,000}$th part of an inch. A single grain may be beaten into a leaf which will cover $56\frac{3}{4}$ inches, or may be drawn into a wire 500 feet in length. Gold is distinguished from nearly all other metals by its extreme density. Its specific gravity (its weight as compared with that of an equal bulk of pure water) is nearly $19\frac{1}{2}$, while that of silver is not quite $10\frac{1}{2}$, lead not quite $13\frac{1}{2}$, and quicksilver no more than $11\frac{1}{2}$. Its greater relative density is of great use in determining its presence when other indications happen to be wanting. Should the miner or washer find a piece of quartz ot more than ordinary weight, he is seldom disappointed in finding it auriferous. Such a test is the more valuable as there are several mineral substances which have a striking resemblance to gold. One of these is the "yellow mica." Dr. Lyon Playfair recently exhibited a specimen of this mineral, part of a cargo brought from the Arkansas in mistake for gold, a mistake which nearly ruined the adventurer who brought it. The same professor tells us that, a short time since, a vessel arrived at a seaport from Ichaboe, having as part of its cargo a number of bags of supposed gold. Two dealers in the precious metals went to examine this supposed treasure. One prudently submitted a specimen to the inspection of a scientific man; but the other, hoping to steal a march upon his fellow trader, went on board in the middle of the night, and bought the whole at a high price, the material being, in a commercial point of view, utterly worthless. It is important to remember, as a chemical test of great simplicity, that gold will dissolve when heated in a mixture of aquafortis and spirits of salts; or "by throwing a little common salt and saltpetre into water, and adding a little oil of vitriol, chlorine will be produced, and the gold will dissolve." The gold thus dissolved can then be brought back to its original state by other processes equally simple.

Gold generally occurs in a pure state, or at least so pure that its metallic character can at once be recognised. Other metals are generally found in combination with foreign substances. Iron, copper, tin, and lead, are most frequently found in chemical combination with oxygen, sulphur, arsenic, and carbon; so that their presence can only be distinguished by a scientific eye; but gold probably in all cases is in a state of mechanical mixture, not chemical combination. It is found most frequently on or near the surface of the earth in veins of quartz or other minerals, from a few inches to several feet in breadth; or else in places not far distant, where it has been carried by the action ot water, and there deposited. From these circumstances spring the various methods of searching for gold. When sought for in its original seat, the quartz veins, the process is very laborious; vast masses of rock have to be removed, and all the arts of *mining* to be resorted to. In other cases the operations are more simple. Where the gold has been drifted by the action of water over the surface of the land, it is generally found to the depth of a few feet, under a cover of soil, peat, sand, gravel, or other materials capable of being washed down from the neighbouring rocks. The removing of this cover in search of the gold underneath constitutes the "*dry diggings;*" the "*wet diggings*" are those which are carried on in the beds of rivers.

Considerable excitement prevails at the present time respecting the probable effect which the rich discoveries in California and Australia will have upon the value of gold, and consequently on the value of fixed incomes. It will aid in forming an intelligent opinion on this subject to know the ratio of our supply of gold, both past and present, to the entire stock of our pecuniary wealth. It is calculated that the whole of the money current in Europe at the time of the discovery of America amounted to £34,000,000. That produced in the interval 1492–1599, after making allowance for the loss by wearing away, probably amounted to £138,000,000, which added to the former gives a total of £172,000,000. It is further calculated that the quantity which during the same period was conveyed to Asia in exchange for its commodities, or applied to other uses, amounted to £42,000,000, leaving the stock of gold and silver coin current in Europe at the end of 1599, £130,000,000. During the interval 1600–1700, our entire supply of gold was derived from America, whose mines are calculated to have produced in the course of the century £337,500,000 worth of the precious metals. Of this, £33,000,000 were sent to the Philippine Islands, India, and China; £60,000,000 of gold were employed in the decorative arts; and if £34,000,000 is allowed for diminution in natural wear, losses by shipwreck, etc., the amount of coined money in Europe at the end of 1699 may be estimated at £297,000,000 sterling. During the next century our chief supplies were drawn from America, the whole of which, including gold dust from Africa, and the gold and silver produce of Europe, may be set down at an aggregate of £800,000,000, or, £8,000,000 annually. During the present century the sources of supply have been more numerous, and some have grown less fertile. The American mines were estimated in 1840 at £5,600,000 a year, a sum very considerably lower than Humboldt's estimate thirty years previous, and their aggregate amount (excluding California, of course) has not increased during the last four or five years. Carolina, Georgia, and other parts of the United States, have produced large quantities of gold, its value having been in 1828, 46,000 dollars, and in 1841, 542,117 dollars. The great increase of gold, however, has been from the Russian mines. In 1830, the gold washings of Siberia produced *five poods;* in 1842, 631 *poods;* a pood being equal to forty pounds troy. In this latter year the total produce of the Russian mines, including those in the Ural Mountains, was 971 poods, or £1,989,128. 11*s*., and sir Roderick Murchison estimates the produce of gold at the present time in Russia at £3,000,000 per annum. California exported gold to this country in 1850 to the value of £700,000, in 1851 to the value of £1,300,000; and if the importation of the present year (1852) goes on at its past rate, it will not be less than £2,000,000. From Australia we received last year £40,000, while to the end of June in this year we received £2,600,000, being at the rate of £5,200,000 a year, an amount not far from equal to the whole produce of the American mines in 1840. Mr. Hunt says, "It has been estimated by some that £23,000,000 of gold and silver will be added to our store of precious metals this year. This appears to be one of the exaggerated statements arising out of the fever of the day: we shall not receive more than £11,000,000 from the United States, California, and Australia; and if we receive £3,000,000 more from all other sources, it will be as much as we may expect."

In asking what effect the increased *supply* of gold will have in raising or lowering its present value, we must not forget to inquire into the state of the *demand*. This side of the question is as important as the former, for though the supply of gold has greatly increased, yet if the demand for it has increased, or is likely to increase in the same ratio, its value will remain undisturbed. We may recognise this more clearly if we select some other article for illustration. If the quantity of wheat, for example, at present in the markets of the world were gradually doubled, the wants of the population remaining the same, its value would be greatly diminished. The holder of wheat to the previous value of £10,000 would find his property diminished probably by more than half that amount, and all payments fixed in wheat would be worth no more than half their former value. But if by any means whatever, when the quantity of wheat was doubled, the demand for it was doubled also, its value would remain unchanged. We estimate the value of money by the quantity of commodities it will purchase, and this is fixed by the quantity of both which happens to be in the market together. If the present amount of commodities purchaseable with money were doubled, or the existing stock of money were reduced by one-half, that portion of the latter which remained would evidently increase in value in the same proportion, and the converse process would take place if the existing sum of all commodities were to be reduced by one-half the present amount, or that of money were doubled. But if both were multiplied or diminished in equal ratio, no change would transpire in their relative value. This is precisely what facts demonstrate to be taking place at the present time. The quantity of gold is being augmented, but an augmentation equally rapid is going on in the quantity of commodities purchaseable with it. We have more money; but our growing commerce and manufactures find it more work to do. Money is the exchanging medium, but we have twice what we formerly had to exchange; to avoid inconvenience, therefore, it is desirable that money should increase to the same extent. The gold produced during the last two years seems to have been entirely absorbed in meeting the demands of commerce. The exportation of coin from England keeps pace with the importation of raw gold. From November, 1850, to June, 1851, the Bank of England issued 9,500,000 sovereigns, being at the rate of 18,000,000 a year; and so great has been the demand for our gold coins, that since November last there have been coined at the Mint 3,500,000 sovereigns and half-sovereigns, and the rate of production can hardly keep pace with the increasing demand. Besides the increased demand for the precious metals which arises thus from their use as money, they are being employed to an unprecedented extent in the arts and manufactures, and this must tend directly to increase the demand. In Birmingham alone, the weekly consumption of pure gold is one thousand ounces; ten thousand ounces are used annually for gilding metals; one establishment in the potteries employs, in gilding porcelain, etc., £3,500, and another nearly £2,000. It is calculated by Mr. McCulloch, that the total annual consumption of the precious metals in the arts is £6,050,000, or more than three-fourths of the entire annual produce of all the mines in the world during the last century. Besides this, nearly £2,000,000 annually are required to make up for waste and loss in the existing metallic currency, so that a supply of £8,000,000 or £9,000,000 is absolutely necessary before any addition can be made to the quantity of the precious metals in circulation. From these facts alone we may conclude "that the influx of Australian and Californian gold will produce but little change in its value in Europe."

One of the most interesting subjects connected with a metallic medium of exchange is COINAGE. In ancient times, gold and silver were sold by weight. Abraham weighed the purchase money of Machpelah, and the sons of Jacob, when they went to purchase corn in Egypt, carried their money "in full weight." In the prophet Amos, the Israelitish merchants are represented as "falsifying the balances by deceit." The shekel and talent do not appear to have been originally fixed and stamped pieces of money, but simply weights used in traffic. Hence the injunction, "Thou shalt not have in thy bag divers weights, a great and a small." It was customary for the Jews to have scales attached to their girdles for weighing the gold or silver they received, but the Canaanites carried them in their hands. Pliny tells us, on the authority of an ancient historian, that until the times of Servius Tullius the

Romans had no coined money, bars of copper being used instead. Long after the reign of William the Conqueror, money was paid into the English exchequer by weight, and in many parts of China and Abyssinia the value of gold and silver is still ascertained in the same manner. The origin of coinage may be accounted for on the most obvious principles. Previous to the reign of William III., it was the sworn duty of a public officer, called an almager, to measure all cloth manufactured in this realm, and to indicate by a mark that it was of a certain required length. Such a step was thought necessary to protect the buyer from imposition; and if really so with an article comparatively inexpensive, the actual quantity of which it was so easy to ascertain, we may conceive how necessary it was felt to have some method of guaranteeing the quality and weight of the precious metals. Without such a guarantee, every purchase into which they entered must have been very slow and precarious, since in every case the seller would have had to ascertain, not only their weight, but whether they contained any mixture of alloy. If this could have been done without much inconvenience in the case of skilled merchants and large transactions, it would be different with the thousand petty exchanges which take place every day between inexperienced or ignorant persons. We cannot doubt, from the ease with which spurious money is circulated even in the face of existing precautions, that if there were no coinage, frauds would be indefinitely multiplied, and a sense of insecurity produced which would soon put an end to one-half our present commerce.

The advantages of coined money led to its adoption at a very early period. At first, perhaps, the process of coining consisted simply in imposing a certain mark upon a piece of metal to certify its quality, leaving its amount to be ascertained by weight; but one improvement leading to another, the processes of assaying and weighing were both dispensed with, by reducing all money to certain denominations, each possessing a fixed and uniform value. Thus, in our own country, that which we now call a pound was originally a pound's weight of silver. This was coined into twenty shillings, and each shilling made exchangeable for twelve silver pennies. It is evident that this further improvement must have been very favourable to commerce, by facilitating the conclusion of every purchase, the exact value of the pecuniary equivalent being settled beforehand. In most countries the prerogative of coining has been assumed by the state, to which it has often been a source of considerable profit. This arose partly from the seigniorage or duty which was charged on all metals passing through the mint; but whatever emoluments might arise from this practice, which is now abolished, they were trivial compared with the immense sums of which the public have been defrauded by the systematic depreciation of the coin. This nefarious course has been taken by the state in almost every country in Europe, whenever its coffers needed replenishing or its debts grew burdensome. It has been said that corporate bodies have no conscience, and the utterer of this maxim could hardly wish a better illustration of its truth than the historic fact to which we advert. If a person owed a hundred pounds while his property was not worth more than fifty pounds, he would be thought dishonest or insane if he proceeded to give his creditors sixpence for every shilling, and to insist upon this as a full payment of his debts. Still more villanous would it be thought if, having the power, he decreed that such a change should be legal throughout the land; that in all future payments sixpence should count for a shilling. This would be nothing less than a robbery upon all who had any money owing them; it would deprive every creditor of one-half his rights. Yet this is precisely what some European governments have done again and again. The injustice has not been perpetrated exactly in the way we have described; this would have been too flagrant; but the same end has been more covertly reached. A piece of silver, which ought to have been coined into, say, two shillings, has been coined into three, and those to whom it was issued at its full nominal value been cheated to the extent of one-third. We have already seen that at the time of the Conquest an English pound consisted of a full pound's weight of silver. This was divided into twenty shillings, and each of these again into twelve silver pennies, each shilling being in weight one-twentieth, and each penny one-hundred-and-fortieth part of the original pound. The coin remained in this state till the days of Edward I., when a depreciation took place, which was continued under successive sovereigns, till, in the time of Elizabeth, a pound of silver was coined into sixty-two shillings, the real value of which was thus three times below its nominal value. Such a course is not peculiar to modern times. Ancient Rome furnishes a remarkable instance. On the first coinage of money under Servius Tullius, the *as*, or *pondo*, contained twelve ounces, but in three hundred years after it was reduced to two ounces, so that a pecuniary engagement fixed at the beginning of that period could be met at its close with one-sixth its original and just amount. France, however, affords the most flagrant instance of this evil on record, since a livre or pound of the days of Charlemagne exceeded by sixty-six times the amount to which it had sunk in 1789. Happily the time has gone by when such oppressive measures could be forced upon the world.

When several kinds of metals are used in money, it is necessary to have one set apart as the LEGAL STANDARD OF VALUE. This will be at once evident if we reflect that the value of the precious metals, in reference to other commodities, depends, as we have seen, entirely upon the quantity in which they can be procured. If the quantity of gold now in circulation were *instantly* doubled, and commodities and purchasers remained as before, its value would at once sink one-half, just as the price of wheat would sink to that extent if the quantity which is stored in the granaries of Europe were suddenly raised to twice its present amount. The same may be affirmed of silver, copper, or any other metal or article whatsoever. Now if gold and silver, in all their fluctuations, always rose or fell in precisely the same ratio—if an ounce of gold, however large or small the quantity of other commodities which could be had in exchange for it, were always worth exactly so many ounces of silver, as far as those metals are concerned, no one standard of value would be required. But we have no security that the ratio of increase or diminution in the two cases will be the same. The discovery of a gold or silver mine might at any time break the balance, and considerably diminish the value of one in relation to another. If, then, by the greater fruitfulness of existing mines, or the discovery of new ones, the quantity of silver in circulation were doubled, a dishonest debtor, by discharging his liabilities in silver, might cheat his creditors out of one-half their claims. In order to prevent the occurrence of such an evil, the legislature in England has constituted gold the only legal tender for all payments above forty shillings.

THE CURRENCY of a country is that portion of its capital which is employed solely as a medium of exchange. We have mentioned reasons which make it preferable that metals should be used as a vehicle of exchange; the chief of which is that they have an actual worth of their own, a sovereign not only indicating value to the amount of twenty shillings, but actually possessing it. There are serious objections, however, to an exclusively metallic currency, arising from its expensiveness. It must be borne in mind that money, so far as it merely serves the purpose of exchange, bears no profit, it adds nothing to the wealth of the country, it serves as a passage for commodities from one person to another, but it does nothing more, and it is quite open to inquiry whether this solitary function could not be discharged in a cheaper way. Assuming the currency of England to be £50,000,000, though the probability is that it is much more, its annual worth at six per cent. interest is three millions, and this consequently is the rent we pay for the use of a passage for the transfer of our goods. But this is not all we pay; the precious metals, though very durable, are yet susceptible of wear and tear. A process of trituration is continually taking place in the transit of money from hand to hand, a palpable proof of which we have in the smooth appearance of coins which have been a long time in use. Besides, a large quantity of coin is frequently lost by fires or shipwreck. It would be a moderate estimate to set down the diminution of the currency in these various ways at half a million annually, which fixes the yearly cost of conducting our exchanges through the medium of the precious metals, at three and a half millions.

One of the advantages of BANKS, considered as public institutions, consists in their lessening the expense of maintaining a metallic currency without any detriment to its great advantages. By their help a large portion of what constitutes the floating capital of the country is employed in remunerative undertakings, and thus increases the aggregate wealth of the community. With dealers of all kinds there are intervals, sometimes considerable, between their purchases. If, during these periods, their money were locked up in a coffer, it would be of no service either to themselves or others. But if, instead of remaining thus inactive, it could be deposited with some person who would give security to pay it again on demand, it might be made, by profitable employment, to bear a high interest, which would go to enrich in certain proportions the owner of the money and the person to whom it was lent. Moreover, if this person was generally known to be a man of integrity and wealth, one, to use a familiar but expressive saying, whose "word is as good as his bond," the money might be left in his hand, and a written promise to pay it on demand might enable the dealer to effect his purchase just as well. This supposed case illustrates the theory of banking. By means of promissory notes, issued in the name of competent individuals, a quantity of gold and silver, equal to their aggregate amount, may be drawn from circulation, and applied to the productive interests of the country. Thus, not only the money which would be dead stock in the hands of the merchant during the intervals of his purchase, but a large portion of that which is required to carry on the business of the nation, may be virtually added to its fixed capital. "The gold and silver money," says Adam Smith, "which circulates in any country, may be compared to a highway, which, while it circulates and carries to market all the grass and corn of the country, itself produces not a single pile of either. The judicious operation of banking, by providing, if I may use so violent a metaphor, a sort of wagon road through the air, enables the country, as it were, to convert a great part of its highways into pastures and corn-fields, and thereby to increase very considerably the produce of its land and labour."

Banks appear to be institutions of great antiquity. Our Lord's allusion, in his parable of the talents, to the neglect of the slothful servant, who did not put his money into *the bank*, from which it might have been received with usury, would seem to favour the supposition, if the words be correctly translated, that in Judæa banks of some kind existed. The exchangers of money, also, who were driven from the temple, seem to have been a class of individuals who performed some of those functions which bankers now exercise. In Greece, the public were in the habit of committing their treasures to the custody of one of their principal temples, which, in times of peril and commotion, was respected from its supposed sacred character. The temple of Delphi was in this manner the great bank of Greece before the time of Homer, and seems to have been proverbial for its riches. At Athens, also, a flourishing trade in banking appears to have been carried on; and a passage occurs in the writings of Xenophon which would seem to imply that the principles on which joint-stock banking in modern times is conducted were not entirely unknown. At Rome bankers existed under the terms *argentarii* and *numularii.* Some of these were appointed by the government to receive the taxes; others carried on business on their own account; and men of wealth paid, as in the present day, their revenues into these establishments, settling their accounts with their creditors by giving a draft or check on the bank. During the middle ages, banking was conducted not unskilfully by the Venetians and the Florentines. The bank of Venice in particular had for many centuries a European celebrity, and was imitated in the year 1609 by the bank of Amsterdam, which, for two centuries, fostered the extensive commerce of Holland.

The business of banking, in the modern acceptation of the term, did not begin in England till the middle of the seventeenth century. It originated with the goldsmiths of London, who, in addition to their trade in bullion, began then both to borrow and lend money. In the former case they gave receipts for the money entrusted to their care, which circulated at their specified value, and thus laid the foundation for the introduction of bank notes. As lenders, they negotiated chiefly with the king, to whom they often advanced the amount of his taxes before they could be collected, thus originating a precedent which was afterwards followed by the Bank of England.

The Bank of England is the largest monetary establishment in the world. It was founded in 1694. Though really a joint-stock company, it has been from its commencement a national rather than a private institution. Its origin may be called political, and marks a most important crisis in the modern history of England. The government which had been established at the Revolution was in want of money. Its circumstances were critical, and therefore its credit poor. The idea of a large banking concern, under state patronage, when suggested by Mr. William Patterson, a Scotch gentleman, was favourably received. A charter was readily granted, and the first subscribed capital, amounting to £1,200,000, was lent to government at the high interest of eight per cent. In three years after, another loan of more than a million was made to government, but this was repaid in 1807. Successive loans, however, have raised the debt on the part of government to the bank to more than eleven millions—a monetary proof that its stability is immeasurably stronger than that of its poorer predecessor a century and a half ago.

By an act of parliament passed in the year 1708, no firm consisting of more than six partners had been allowed to carry on the business of banking in England. No public institution arose in consequence to compete with the Bank of England; and for a century and a quarter, the monetary business of the country was conducted by that establishment, in conjunction with a number of private bankers. The large and extensive failures, however, which had taken place among the latter, led, in the year 1826, to the repeal of the law of 1708, and banks with an unlimited number of partners, commonly called joint-stock banks, were allowed to be established, subject only to the proviso that none established within sixty-five miles of London should be allowed to issue their own notes. Banks of this description had been opened in Scotland cotemporaneously with the foundation of the Bank of England, and by the prudence of their management had obtained the confidence of the country. The circumstances which gave many of them special security was the fact that the property of all the shareholders was liable for all the engagements of the company.

Early in the present century, savings' banks, intended more especially for the benefit of the humbler classes of society, were introduced, receiving deposits of sums which were too small to be lodged in other establishments, and encouraged the depositors by giving a rate of interest somewhat higher than could be obtained elsewhere. They have proved of great advantage to the community, having been the means of introducing economy and providence into the habits of the people, improving their morals, increasing their means, and engaging their interest in the support of public order.

It is interesting to remark, that of the private banks which are established throughout the country, the three London firms of Child's, Hoare's, and Snow's, are even older than the Bank of England. The number of private banks in London in 1848 were seventy-four; and the amount of money transactions carried on chiefly through them is estimated at nearly five millions daily. "In 1840, according to a pamphlet on the subject by the late Mr. Leatham, of Wakefield, the returns of the clearing-house, an establishment in which the accounts of twenty-seven London bankers are daily balanced, amounted to the enormous sum of £975,000,000."

The establishment just mentioned is one of the most remarkable exemplifications of the system of modern banking. It was set on foot in 1770 by the private bankers, and is intended to economize both money and labour in the settlement of their mutual accounts. "The cheques and bills of exchange on the authority of which a great part of the money paid and received by bankers is exchanged, are taken from each of the clearing bankers to the clearing-house several times in the day, and the cheques and bills drawn on one banker are cancelled by those he holds on others." Mr. Tate, in his "System of the London Bankers' Clearances Explained and Exemplified," tells us that "the rapidity with which the last charges require to be entered, and the bustle created by their swift distribution through the room are difficult to be conceived. It is when on the point of striking four, and on days of heavy business, that the beauty of the alphabetical arrangement of the clearer's desk is to be seen. All the distributors are moving in the same direction round the room, with no further interference than may arise from the more active pressing upon or outstripping the slower of their fellow-assistants. With equal celerity are their last credits entered by the clearers. A minute or two having passed, all the noise has ceased. The deputy-clearers have left with the last charges on their houses; the clearers are silently occupied in casting up the amounts of the accounts in their books, balancing them, and entering the differences in their balance-sheets, until at length announcements begin to be heard of the probable amounts to be received or paid as a preparation for the final settlement. The four o'clock balances having been entered in the balance sheet, each clearer goes round to check and mark off his accounts with the rest, with 'I charge you,' or 'I credit you,' according as each balance is in his favour or against him."

In the banking system of a mercantile community, we reach the highest possible point of refinement in the medium of exchange. What a contrast is presented, for example, between those bars of gold which were weighed to the merchant in ancient times, and the modern bank note! How clumsy the one! what a triumph of ingenuity and skill the other! They may be taken, not inappropriately, as the respective symbols of barbarism and civilization. Let the reader take a five-pound Bank of England note from his pocket-book, and attentively examine it. Mark its thinness; the finest writing-paper is clumsy when compared with it. Hold it up to the light, and it is almost transparent. But though so thin, it is nevertheless characterized by a roughness of texture which alone would enable an experienced clerk to test the genuineness of notes passing through his hand as rapidly as another could count them. Next we have the water-mark. This is incorporated in the very texture of the paper, and is effected by a certain arrangement of wires in the mould in which the pulp is taken up. No art has ever yet been able to counterfeit the bevelled edges which distinguish three sides of every Bank of England note. Here, if nowhere else, the plans of the forger are sure to suffer shipwreck. "No one can have failed to remark the exceeding strength of the notes of the Bank of England. The wear they are capable of enduring is astonishing. For the purpose of accumulating the strain to which a note in circulation is liable, so as to represent in one quality its power of resisting tension, we may secure the edges of a piece of banking paper of the size and figure of a note, and then load its surface. Such a piece of paper weighs, before sizing, seventeen and a half grains, and in this state it will support without tearing a weight of thirty-six pounds. The size subsequently added weighs one grain, and its addition enables the note to sustain a strain of twenty pounds more, or, in all fifty-six pounds,—half a hundred-weight."*

But great as is the difference between the rude ingots which formerly constituted the only medium of traffic, and the modern bank note, the moral sentiments they seem respectively to embody, present us with a still wider contrast. In this light, bullion is the emblem of barbarism, and paper of civilization. The one reminds us of suspicion and distrust; we see the merchant carefully guarding his goods till he has secured the golden equivalent, refusing to part with a single article till he has deposited in his coffers a tangible *quid pro quo*. Imagine the Israelites who carried spices into Egypt offering the sons of Jacob a promissory note! How punctually would such a bond have been honoured by the lawless coursers of the desert! It is civilization alone, as exhibited in the ascendency of law and honour,

* Lectures on "The Manufacture of Bank of England Notes," by Rev. J. Barlow, M.A.

which gives to written engagements a current value; and when we find a merchant willing to empty his warehouse in return for a scrap of paper, we feel that the world must have advanced immensely in the practice of political and social virtues.

The whole history of bank notes is indeed an exceedingly curious one. In all probability the bill of exchange was their predecessor, and suggested their use. By the former document, a person who wished to transmit money to a distance was enabled to do so, on procuring an order from a merchant, drawn upon another merchant residing at or near the place where the money was to be paid. When it was found however, that an easy and portable order of this kind could be obtained, the man possessing it, if he was satisfied of the responsibility of the individuals by whom the bill was signed, would prefer retaining it rather than encumber himself with specie, of which he might be plundered. He would in time, perhaps, pay away the document to others, and they too, if they were satisfied with the names upon it, might prefer holding it instead of specie, until it suited their convenience to demand payment of it. That this was the precursor of our bank note system is proved indeed by inspecting some of the first bills of exchange issued by the Bank of England, which appear to have passed from hand to hand in the manner above described, and to have supplied the place of the regular bank note. In some of the manufacturing districts of England, indeed, at the present day, bills of exchange, instead of being kept till due, still perform the part of a circulating medium, and supply to a considerable extent the office of bank notes.

Bank notes appear to have been known in China long before they were introduced into Europe.* It appears that, B.C. 119, to meet the increased revenues of the state, skin notes were introduced by a skilful Chinese minister of finance, being pieces of leather made from the skins of white deer bred in a park round the royal palace. At a later period, notes made from the bark of the paper mulberry were also in extensive circulation in China. In England, those issued by the Bank of England seem to have been the first bank notes, properly so called, of which we have any trace. No fixed amount appears to have been determined on, as the minimum or maximum of each note. Some years ago, indeed, the newspapers of the day stated that a note for *sixpence*, issued more than a hundred years ago at a time when there was a great scarcity of copper coinage, was discovered and presented at the bank. For a long period, however, a pound was the lowest sum for which notes were issued; but at present, except in Scotland

* In a number of the "Chinese Repository" for June, 1851, an interesting description of a modern Chinese note is given. It is stated to be rather larger than a Bank of England note—is printed on stout paper made from the bamboo—and is covered with various stamps, seals, and written characters, to prevent forgery.

and Ireland, no note of a less amount than five pounds can be put forth.*

Great as are the advantages of a paper currency, yet it is not without some serious drawbacks, for at various periods individuals and establishments issuing bank notes have done so to a greater extent than they had the means of easily paying in gold. In 1792, 1814, 1815, 1816, 1825, and 1826, England sustained, from the failures of private banking establishments, an amount of bankruptcy and misery that has never perhaps been equalled, except by the breaking up of the Mississippi scheme in France.† In the year 1797, the Bank of England itself was placed by government in circumstances which led to one of the most remarkable passages in the monetary history of this country. The war with France had produced a great scarcity of money, and distrust having extensively prevailed, apprehensions were entertained that the Bank, if hard pressed, might itself be unable to meet its engagements. Parliament, however, having investigated its affairs, and found that it possessed property to the extent of nearly sixteen millions, the Bank Restriction Act was passed, the effect of which was that the public had not the power if they wished of demanding gold in exchange for Bank of England notes. For the

* Visitors are shown in the Bank of England a cancelled note for one million of pounds sterling. It appears to have been used in the transactions between the Bank and the government.

† McCulloch's "Commercial Dictionary"—Article, *Banks*.

first three years after the passing of this Act, the issues of the Bank were so moderate that the notes not only kept on a par with gold, but actually bore a small premium. In 1810, however, they had been issued to such an extent that they were discounted at thirteen per cent., that is, if a party required a hundred sovereigns to send out of England, he would have been obliged to have paid for them one hundred and thirteen Bank of England one-pound notes. Many attempts were made to prevent this depreciation, but they proved ineffectual. In 1819, accordingly, sir Robert, then Mr. Peel, brought into parliament a bill, repealing the Bank Restriction Act, and rendering it compulsory on the Bank of England to pay its notes in gold upon demand. This Act did not, however, take effect till 1821.

Great distress certainly followed the readjustment of the currency, and extensive failures also took place. The whole question as to the propriety or otherwise of the measure has been much argued, and the result is thus summed up by Mr. McCulloch :—" One party contends that Mr. Peel's Act not only put an end to those fluctuations in the value of money which had previously been productive of great mischief, and gave effect to the solemn engagements into which the public had entered with the national creditor, but that it did this without adding materially to the nation's burdens. But another, and perhaps a more numerous party, take a totally different view of this measure.

They contend that the public was not bound to return to cash payments at the old standard at the termination of the war; that the return has very greatly enhanced the value of the currency; and that this enhancement, by adding proportionably to the fixed burdens laid on the industrious classes, has been most injurious to their interests. It will be found, however," adds Mr. McCulloch, in conclusion, "that in this, as in most other cases of the sort, the statements of both parties have been exaggerated, and that if, on the one hand, the measure has not been so advantageous as its apologists represent, neither, on the other, has it been nearly so injurious as its enemies would have us believe."

In consequence of the disasters more or less attributable to a paper currency, various remedies have been proposed by financial writers to obviate them. By some, the power to issue notes has been proposed to be limited to one bank established by government, whose responsibility would be undoubted; but to this it has been replied, that such an establishment would speedily become an instrument of political oppression, and in times of panic and public calamity would cause, in the event of public credit being assailed, universal disaster, a result which would be avoided were the power of issuing notes left, as at present, to several establishments, all of whom would be unlikely to suspend payment at one time. By other economists it has been proposed that banks should be made to lodge with government security for their notes issued, so that the public might be thus protected. Sir Robert Peel, however, by his celebrated Bill of 1844, took the most important step which had perhaps ever been adopted in reference to the currency question in this country. With a view to prevent the excessive over-issue of notes, it was enacted that the existing banks should not in future issue notes beyond the amount which they had, on an average, in circulation at the time of the passing of the Act. The total amount of notes which could be issued by all the establishments in the country was eventually limited as follows :—

Bank of England	£14,000,000*
Joint Stock Banks . . .	5,009,020
Private Banks in England .	3,469,872
Banks in Scotland . . .	3,087,209
Banks in Ireland	6,354,494

The policy of this celebrated measure of sir R. Peel has been disputed by many. Its inconvenience was certainly evinced during the year 1847, when the Bank of England having reached its full power of issue, a panic ensued,

* These amounts are extracted from the "Bankers' Magazine" for 1846. The amount of the Private Banks and Joint Stock Banks' issue is now perhaps somewhat less, as some banks have since the date of the return withdrawn from business.
The Bank of England, in addition to its £14,000,000 of circulation, can also issue when necessary to an unlimited extent, provided, to meet such additional issue, it has in its coffers four-fifths of gold and one-fifth of silver.

which was only relieved upon the government permitting the Bank to issue notes, if needful, beyond the amount fixed by law. Desirable as it is to avoid all injurious excesses of paper currency, it is held by the opponents of sir Robert's measure that it is neither desirable nor safe to restrict the credit operations of a large commercial country like this within fixed limits; and that by thus contracting within certain artificial bounds the power of banks to assist their customers, an injury is done to the progress of the community. These writers also contend that the tendency of banks to issue an undue quantity of notes is sufficiently counteracted by the certainty with which notes so issued fall into the hands of other banks, by whom payment of them is demanded in gold. Communities, like individuals, it is likewise alleged, must be taught in the selection of banks or bank notes to exercise that care and vigilance which protects them in ordinary matters; for governments, as it has been well observed, may nurse, by undue legislation, nations into a state of weakness. There is, perhaps, a peculiar danger of this in a matter like the currency, which is of a nature so intricate as to be understood by only comparatively a small number of those most interested in its due regulation. Whatever be the truth of these views, it must be admitted that when the magnitude of interests involved is considered, too much care cannot be taken to place upon a solid foundation the banking institutions of a country. The legislature has made a wise movement for this purpose lately. It has ordered the names of all the members of the firm composing a private bank, and those of all the shareholders in joint-stock banks, to be published in the newspapers of districts where business is carried on by them. The public can thus at any time satisfy themselves, if they exercise only proper caution, as to the responsibility of the parties to whom their money is committed.

CHAPTER V.

THE MORALS OF MONEY: THE FALLACIES AND FAILINGS OF MONIED MEN.

Hitherto we have contemplated money from an exclusively secular point of view—we now proceed to view it under the higher aspect of its moral and spiritual relations. This is no arbitrary change of topic—no piece of *finesse*, adopted in order to surprise the reader into a sermon, but the ascent of a natural climax. Everything on earth points to eternity; every object, every pursuit, has its spiritual side—that on which it adjoins the soul, and silently works itself into its immortal texture. God has attached to every condition in life its own set of influences. Everything we see or do, or think or say, has a moral power attached to it: our talents, opportunities, privileges, joys; our daily tasks, duties, trials; the hopes, anxieties, disappointments, and successes of business; the annoyances and irritations of the world, the temptations to sin and the incentives to holiness which surround our path; the advantages and disadvantages of our social position; our soberest reflections, our most mirthful sallies, our very fancies and day-dreams;—all are laden with lasting results, all are silently exerting some influence on our everlasting state. Yes, ETERNITY is seen as a Divine handwriting on everything that meets the eye—on the exchange, the factory, and the warehouse, as well as the temple and the tomb.

Here is an article of faith of which most men need to be more heartily convinced. It is the chief point in the practical creed of life. The worldly principle in human nature loves to separate time from eternity—loves to view this world and the next as two entirely separate spheres, having no vital connexion with each other. We speak with horror, and justly so, of infidelity—that which denies the Bible, looks upon the soul as mortal, or merely as a part of the Infinite, and questions the evidence of a personal Deity. Such sentiments are dark and sinful beyond measure, but it may be doubted whether they are more mischievous to the interest of Christianity than that poisonous scepticism which so many cherish without misgiving; that which practically denies the presence and claims of God in the business of daily life; which views wealth as exclusively of the individual's own getting, to be placed at the beck of selfishness or caprice, without a single remonstrance of conscience for the neglect of any obligation, whether to God or man. Such infidelity is truly a bane to the soul, a canker to the church, and a curse to the world.

If, as we have shown in previous pages, there is a very powerful tendency in society, according to its natural constitution as founded by the Creator, to become richer, we cannot imagine that riches are unavoidably and necessarily hostile to virtue. This would be to impeach the moral character of the Divine government. The evils of riches must therefore lie in the mode in which they are gained or used. Every tendency which is *necessarily* developed in social progress must be favourable to the spiritual interests of mankind. Poverty has often been lauded as the state which is most propitious to the moral excellence of individuals and communities; yet everybody shuns poverty, everybody is so constituted that he naturally wishes to escape it, and the direct effect of prudence, industry, and their kindred virtues, is to accumulate wealth. On this ground alone we might pronounce beforehand with the most absolute certainty, that poverty has no peculiar patent for goodness, and that growth in wealth does not necessarily involve a deterioration of the moral character. The great empires of antiquity are often adduced in supposed confirmation of an opposite view. We are told of the virtues which marked the infancy, as contrasted with the universal degeneracy of manners that characterized the meridian of the Roman empire. But the reference is useless. In the first place, it is questionable whether the Rome of Romulus could be taken as a higher exemplar of public virtue than the Rome of Cæsar. Its vices were of a different kind, but they were vices still. If it is lawful to discern anything substantial among the shadows of Livy, we may find in the very earliest period of the Roman state innumerable traces of injustice, violence, and sensuality, which have no point of contrast, save that of coarseness, with those moral enormities which afterwards distinguished the capital of the world. But the vices of imperial Rome must not be ascribed to its wealth; they are due rather to the mode in which its wealth was acquired, and the depraved habits which were connected with it. Its wealth was the fruit of conquest; it was the spoiling of the nations, not the self-elaborated product of capital and industry. It was acquired in a way which developed the sensual and destructive passions, and thus excavated a mine beneath, which at length blew the empire into atoms. Wealth, when acquired by manufactures and commerce, always presupposes the actual exercise of a large amount of useful qualities; and the discipline which must be submitted to in its acquisition, especially when seconded by the influence of religion, affords, within certain limits, a guarantee for continued moral improvement. It may be almost affirmed that commercial affluence can neither be gained nor kept by a people socially corrupt. Empires which owed their greatness to conquest, often sank beneath their own weight; but there is, probably, no instance in which a great commercial state has fallen through the *enervating influence* of pomp and luxury. Nineveh and Babylon, like Rome in after times, were the product of successful war, and fell with the empires whose greatness they represented; Tyre, the mercantile metropolis of the ancient world, was twice permitted by Providence, as a punishment for its pride, to be subdued by powerful invaders; but so far was it from falling to pieces in consequence of internal decay, that after its overthrow by Nebuchadnezzar the energy of its inhabitants soon restored it to its former grandeur, and enabled it to hold out for seven months against the conquering arms of Alexander the Great. Its sins were selfishness and pride, the besetting sins of the strong; the besetting sins, may we not fear, of Britain in this the era of its greatest power, and which, unless our wealth and greatness are sanctified to objects of benevolence and piety, will draw upon us a chastisement no less signal than that of Tyre of old.

Not only is wealth not necessarily hostile to piety, but it is in some respects decidedly propitious to its growth. It affords room for gratitude, furnishes themes for thankful praise, enables the mind to acquiesce in the Divine goodness, without those gigantic efforts of faith which are necessary to recognise his blessings when sent to us in the guise of adversity, and thus makes it an easier task to wave the censer of thankfulness before the seat of mercy. It places us in a position more favourable for the formation of impartial views respecting the character of God's providential economy, inasmuch as it tends to drive from the horizon of our experience those dark clouds through which we are in danger of viewing every portion of the universe. By rendering the heart more joyous, it gives room for the growth of qualities which are often crushed by poverty; kindliness, confidence, general sympathy, faith in the beneficent tendency of the Divine arrangements. Besides, money will purchase books, scientific instruments, and professional aid, thus promoting the work of self-improvement; while the freedom it brings from those solicitudes which relate to the first necessities of life, afford more leisure for the cultivation of pursuits which are not earthly. It will not be disputed that these are points in which the wealthy man has a decided advantage over his poorer neighbour, and this is sufficient to show that the social condition to which mankind are being wafted by the gales of industry, is as friendly to moral excellence as it is undoubtedly to physical enjoyment.

The moral evils of wealth are, we may further observe, greater in a poor than a rich country, and will continually diminish as wealth itself becomes more diffused. Diminish the distance between the various members of society; render refinement, elegance, and plenty common things; make "gold," to give a figurative sense to the literal description which the historian gives us of the greatness of Solomon, "as plenteous as stones, and cedar trees as the sycamore trees for abundance," and you diminish their corrupting power. There is no necessary connexion between wealth and sensual indulgence. Among our most affluent merchants we might find the hardest workers, the clearest, firmest, manliest minds in the whole community; and though the person who merely enjoys the wealth which has been handed down to him from his ancestors, without knowing anything of the wholesome discipline of acquisition, is more exposed to the enervating influence of luxury, how many could be pointed out among the noblest and richest members of our aristocracy, who *use* their property with a master's hand, remaining themselves vigorous and incorrupt, presenting such a blending of elegance and severity as no age or country has produced in greater perfection than our own.

It is also worthy of remark, that the two wealthiest nations of the world are those in which religion is most powerful as an element of social life. England and the United States are the two most Protestant countries on the globe; in them the Bible is free, the preacher of the gospel moves unfettered, piety is welcomed to the domestic hearth, and joins with learning and science in shedding there her benignant lustre; philanthropic institutions rear their heads, and like the tree of life extend their healing shadow over the human race: yet these countries stand highest in point of wealth, and their wealthiest citizens furnish the Christian church with some of its most enlightened and devoted members. In both countries, moreover, the growth of wealth has been unprecedently rapid. Never before in the history of the world was so vast an accumulation gathered in so short a time. If wealth is necessarily unfriendly to religion, we might have expected that the latter would have been overwhelmed ere this by a flood of worldliness, that every trace of spiritual verdure would have become extinct. Instead of this we have beheld during the same period a revival of vital godliness which has kept pace with our social improvement. Our missionary institutions, Bible and Tract Societies, have all commenced since we began our money-making career. Buildings devoted to the worship of God and the instruction of the rising race have sprung up by thousands in our manufacturing districts, and the town whose name is most prominently associated with an order of things which has been ignorantly reviled as an economy of selfishness and irreligion, recently gave a manifestation of specifically Christian benevolence which the world could not rival. Yes, the historian of the nineteenth century will not forget to relate that when queen Victoria visited that part of her dominions, Manchester assembled from beneath the shadow of its factories seventy thousand Sunday School children, and ten thousand teachers, all bound together by a simply religious tie, and presenting an unanswerable proof that the acquisition of wealth may be associated with an enlightened and practical piety.

But wealth, though not necessarily hostile to piety, has nevertheless its special dangers; its besetting fallacies and besetting sins, justifying those solemn warnings to its possessors which are scattered through the word of God. With a friendly hand we will endeavour to lay open a few of both classes to the notice of the reader. One of the fallacies of wealth consists in giving too uniformly a moral character to the successes and reverses of life—in tacitly regarding riches as a virtue and poverty as a crime. Now we admit that the hand of the diligent maketh rich, and that the drunkard and the glutton shall come to poverty; but riches may sometimes proceed from other causes than diligence, and poverty may not always have had the antecedents of drunkenness and gluttony. Poverty, it is also true, may often be traced up to moral causes which throw the entire responsibility upon the individual who is the subject of it. How many persons who are now in utter destitution might have lived in competence, if they had only been prudent and industrious at the outset of their career! They look with envy upon successful men, and talk as though some malignant destiny kept them down, forgetting that their own failure may be justly attributed to themselves. Neglecting to "stir up" their peculiar talents, to develop their mental powers, to seize every opportunity of advancement, and to make those sacrifices which were demanded by a regard to their permanent welfare, some individuals revolve perpetually round the starting-post of life, instead of making a vigorous and determined effort to reach the goal. In such cases poverty is a fault, and the inconveniences it brings may justly be regarded in the light of a retribution. But how many exceptions do we find to this rule! The race is not always to the swift, nor the battle to the strong; the lot is cast into the lap, but the whole disposing thereof is of the Lord. We perform but a humble part in the economy of life. It is ours to seize the opportunity, but who gives it? We must recognise here a mightier Hand. Every person who has attained success is able to recall many circumstances which favoured his rise, without which, for anything he can see, the strength of a Hercules would have been in vain. At best he has been only a co-worker. If he has contributed one element, God has contributed far more. But he is less even than this, since those very talents which enabled him to lay open his sails so as to catch the propitious influences of wind and weather came down from the Father of lights, whose goodness to him is but ill repaid by indulging in judicial severity towards those to whom those talents have been denied.

Another fallacy into which wealth is apt to betray us, is that of making it a virtual synonym of respectability. "A respectable man," in ordinary parlance is apt to mean one who commands so much money. A reference to character is included in the definition, but only to a trivial extent. In forming our estimate, the first idea which presents itself is that of his being "well to do;" the second, that of his possessing a certain measure of excellence. It is to be feared that thousands give this second idea a very feeble recognition. Their ordinary conception of respectability rises no higher than an elegant mansion, and goes no deeper than a suit of rich clothing. Perhaps no association which links two thoughts together is absolutely unreasonable, and in the instance before us it is easy to trace the process of silent argumentation by which we apply the epithet "respectable" to the monied man. Generally speaking, qualities which are truly respectable produce money. We have seen how directly intelligence, sobriety, and the cycle of kindred virtues tend to affluence. This has been observed through many ages, and mankind, transferring to the effect that which properly belongs to the cause, constitute affluence itself an object of respect. Another consideration must enter into an impartial solution. Mankind worship power. To this, under whatever form embodied, all bend the knee. But money is power; there is nothing which money will not purchase, and he who can command an unlimited supply, is clothed with a kind of social omnipotence. These grounds of respect should be duly recognised, but there is one far brighter, one which is independent of outward condition, and may be found within a mud cottage as well as in a royal palace. Goodness alone has a sovereign title to respect. In God this attribute becomes sublime, the very radiance of his ineffable splendour; to Him accordingly we owe absolute homage, and wherever we behold the faintest reflection of it in human character our hearts should meet it with love and reverence. The highest esteem should be grounded entirely on moral and spiritual worth, and of this money is no test whatever. A person may be hypocritical, selfish, profligate, and yet rich; and another sincere, disinterested, godly, and yet poor. All those qualities which entitle to respect may be found without money; and all those which deserve to be branded with execration may be found with it. If we are about to enter upon some great commercial enterprise, a person who can place a large sum of money at our disposal is of course entitled to more consideration than one who is not possessed of a shilling; but when the question is, whom shall we pronounce "respectable," whom shall we inwardly honour, we must add no other principles, we must look at the man himself. If the excellent of the earth were to be gathered together and ranged promiscuously before our eyes, we should probably see represented to us in garb and manners every social and professional variety of the human race; but to the eye of God, who seeth not as man seeth, all would be alike beautiful; —rich and poor, learned and illiterate, would lose their mutual differences in the grand distinction of being the "children of the Highest."

We may mention as another illustration of the class of fallacies to which we allude, an exaggerated conception of the reconciling power of habit. How commonly do we hear it observed, in reference to any exhibition of physical wretchedness, "Ah, poor creatures! but they are used to it;" and how often has such a sentiment proved a bar both to assistance and sympathy! There is as usual some truth in this remark. Such observations are not raised to the rank of maxims without some reason. Providence kindly ordains that we become less susceptible to any inconvenience the longer we bear it; habit is a mitigator of human woe; the burden fits itself to the shoulder, and at length is borne easily. But there are limits to the power of habit. It cannot destroy the strongest susceptibilities of human nature; it cannot reverse instinct, or make misery an element of happiness. An exotic plant may be acclimated, but there is constant war between its own tendencies and its new position, and a degree of inclemency which will kill it. How many human exotics have perished in the process of acclimation! How many who survive drag out a life of suffering! It is not true that man is "a bundle of habits." He has a native force, certain definite appliances within himself, with which outward circumstances are incongruous or otherwise. By being always situated in the same condition he may be ignorant of the pains or pleasures which spring from contrast, but surely it is not necessary to have tasted a higher degree of happiness in order to feel that wretchedness is wretched. Man is not such a thing of experience. Whether conscious of it or not, whoever exists in a state of physical destitution must possess far less than the average of human enjoyment.

Besides those dangers which beset wealth on the side of the intellect, there are others which belong more to the province of the heart. One of these arises from the tendency there is in those pursuits which accumulate wealth to produce an engrossing spirit of worldliness; such an ardent attachment to the things of this life, and such a determination to possess them, as leaves no room for the love of nobler objects. In this respect, the man who is rapidly rising in temporal circumstances is exposed to much greater peril than those who are already wealthy. It is air in motion which constitutes the hurricane; when at rest, whatever within ordinary limits its density may be, we move in it without inconvenience. The passion for wealth may be compared to that of the gamester. At first comparatively feeble, it increases in intensity, till at length the soul is carried away with the fury of a whirlwind. How many a person in the early years of his mercantile career manifested decided indications of a religious spirit; feeling, fresh and vernal, expanded itself in blossoms of spiritual promise. To such a one the Saviour might have uttered those words, so full of hope and fear, "Thou art not far from the kingdom of heaven." But his enterprises began to be unusually successful, and his anxieties were turned into a new channel. Tried on a wider scale, his plans proved in a corresponding degree more lucrative, and proportionably greater force was infused into the worldly tendencies of his heart. At length he had left his former sphere; he had unconsciously wandered into a new orbit. Outwardly his position might be where it formerly was. The same pew in the sanctuary witnessed, at least *once* on the Lord's day, the same decorous recognition of Christian ordinances, the same liberality was exhibited in contributing to the sustenance of evangelical efforts, all the conventional marks by which a Christian man is distinguished from others were duly found among the externals of his life; yet he was essentially another man. The springs of religious sensibility were quite dried up; his very conscience was secularized. "Of the earth, earthy," might be seen written on the rubbish-pyramid of his ambition, and the final issue, kept from its complete fulfilment by a few remaining years, might be expressed in one word,—LOST, to God and to himself.

Nothing can equal in subtlety the first encroachments of a worldly spirit. It assumes the most attractive disguise. Is not diligence in business enforced upon us by a Divine command? Is not negligence in providing for the temporal welfare of our families placed among the practical denials of the Christian faith? Are not the institutions of trade and commerce of Divine appointment? Is not the successful manufacturer or merchant a benefactor to mankind? Such are the specious arguments by which the first overtures of the world are sustained, but they are soon laid aside. Sin, when in comparative abeyance, will consent to knock at the door of the heart; to play the Jesuit and the cringer by turns, in order to get admittance; but, once inside, it will not consent to remain there a moment except on the footing of its own sovereignty. Any course deliberately entered upon and persevered in for a lengthened period, though at first it was at variance with our convictions, and forced us to battle with one-half our moral nature, will at length conciliate the affections, master the will, and enthrone itself in the midst of its conquests, like the strong man armed "keeping his goods in peace." No evil spirit is more bland in its professions, more promising in its appearance, or more imperious in its rule, than that of worldliness; nor is there a more impregnable position within the temporal precincts of the abyss of ruin than that which is occupied by the worldly man. The persecutor, the debauchee, the idolater, may be made a disciple of Christ more easily than he. "It is easier for a camel to go through the eye of a needle, than for a rich man (one who loves riches supremely) to enter into the kingdom of God."

Since wealth is prone to foster misconception

respecting the character and deserts of others, it has also a tendency to affect injuriously our conduct towards them. This tendency, we need not repeat, is far from being necessary; it is not inseparable from wealth; the richest man may be the brightest exemplar of social virtue; but it is at least a tendency which is as incident to an inferior position in life. Amongst the most conspicuous manifestations of this tendency are pride and arrogance; the inward sentiment of superiority, nursed into insolent rigour, dwelt in, gloated on by self-esteem; and the outward expression of that sentiment through the medium of our words and actions. The proud man loves to isolate himself from others, as though he were cast in a more exquisite fashion, or made of more costly materials. He never looks at his fellow-creatures except through a set of lenses, the sole product of his own misled imagination, which diminishes them to the size of pigmies, and turns himself into a sort of Jupiter amongst mortals. Every word and gesture is expressive of contempt, or of a condescension which is still more repulsive. Pride is often found mixed up with feelings of a meaner kind; a subservient ambition, which sedulously courts notice of all who occupy a higher station, and makes every advance the occasion of disowning every species of intercourse with those beneath. How melancholy and ignoble does such a spirit render life! All the honest and generous friendships which bloom to-day, withered to-morrow by the merciless wand of wealth. Those whose countenance was once coveted as an honour, severed at once from our very memories because we grasp a few more lumps of gold, or the smiles of human favour beam upon us with softer benignancy. Ah! wealth is a curse indeed if it make the heart thus unfaithful and dishonest!—if it subordinate our attachment to the wise and excellent to worldly consequence and fame!—if it tempt us to sacrifice upon a heap of gold dust such imperishable jewels as love, honour, constancy, and gratitude!

It is difficult to say whether, in describing the characteristic qualities of pride and arrogance, we should brand them as foolish or pernicious. In a very high degree they are both. That must be pernicious which separates man from man, steels the heart against all sympathy, and makes an immortal being the victim of the most puerile hopes and fears. That must be foolish which provokes ridicule, is its own tormentor, and justifies itself by the very arguments which pronounce its censure. Pride is a blind passion—the precursor of destruction to individuals and states; it is the soul of faction and the spring of discontent; it inflicts incalculable evils on all who fall beneath its power, and, by silently relaxing the social ties, tends to precipitate society into ruin. As cherished by one man towards another it is absurd. Since every good gift comes from God, they who have the costliest gifts are the greatest debtors, and ought to discharge their obligations to the common Parent by treating more kindly those of his offspring whom he has favoured in a less eminent degree. Besides, all men possess in germ the same illustrious faculties. Over all the Eternal bends in infinite pity; for all the Saviour died; all are invited to the honour of being kings and priests unto God, and reigning with him for ever.

There is another sin which is scarcely less despicable and pernicious than pride; we refer to one which is by no means confined to circles of wealth, though it is there most mischievous in its results. The vanity of display is not monopolized, alas! by any section of the community. How many sacrifice their health and run into debt to "keep up an appearance!" How many among the poorer classes neglect real wants to supply fancied ones! But when the same weakness rules a person of extensive resources, a severe blow is inflicted upon the community. His wealth is part of the national stock; he is morally one of a body of trustees, comprising a few thousands, upon whom the employment and well-being of the entire population depend. On public grounds he ought to devote the smallest possible portion of his income to mere luxury, that he may have the more to invest in remunerative enterprise, and the more to give in works of charity and mercy. Economy need not be parsimonious, nor prudence beggarly. The fine arts and costly species of manufacture depend upon the patronage of men of wealth, and patronage exerted in this direction is not without a powerful moral influence upon society. But even the artistic passion must be kept within reasonable limits, and he is no right steward of his wealth who lavishes a hundred thousand pounds in the formation of a picture gallery, when the neighbouring population are starving for want of the capital necessary to make their labour productive, or Christian enterprises languish for support.

Besides these evils which originate in the moral tendency of wealth, there are some which lie more immediately in its use. One of these, lying within the sphere of business, we must be permitted to single out from among the rest for special notice,—we refer to undue SPECULATION. This is entitled to a bad pre-eminence among other sins of business on account of the too favourable light in which it is often regarded, and the appalling consequences which sometimes flow from it. Speculation, when pursued to an extent beyond a person's means, is as foreign to the sober habits of business as the pursuits of the gambler. It stakes success, not on prudence and industry, but in probabilities only a step above chance. It turns trade into a game of hazard, and spreads a feeling of uncertainty and insecurity far and wide. Its moral influence is excessively injurious. The spirit it fosters is as different from that honest emulation which springs from a laudable desire tc succeed in life, as the delirium of a fever from the elastic energy of a healthy man. It is essentially plotting, greedy, secret, overreaching, and easily slides into recklessness regarding the interests of others. Its effects, in an economical point of view, have often been most fatal. How many thousands have been ruined by it! How many volumes might be filled with melancholy narratives of individuals who were hurled in a moment from affluence to poverty, but who might have continued wealthy had they only been contented with the results of honourable exertion! It is too little to say that a person is imprudent who thus risks his all; he has no *right* to do it; he has no right to expose himself and family to the loss which may ensue, nor yet to expose others to the fluctuation and peril which must in any case be the result. One great lesson on the evils of undue speculation has been taught the present generation which will not be speedily forgotten. The public and private disasters of 1847, consequent in a great measure on the railway mania, are still fresh in the recollection of all. The prospect of immediate wealth without the trouble of working for it, led multitudes to change their property for railway shares, thus creating an unnatural demand, and consequent high prices, which soon fell, and involved hundreds in ruin. What an impressive comment do such consequences read upon the declaration of holy writ—"They that *will be* rich fall into temptation and a snare!" 1 Tim. vi. 9. Might not prudence itself inscribe over our marts of business, and at the head of our ledgers, the sentiment of the wise man, "He that hasteth to be rich hath an evil eye, and considereth not that poverty shall come upon him?" Prov. xxviii 22.

There are methods of employing wealth even more sinful and pernicious than speculation, and among these we cannot hesitate to class *every attempt to turn it into an engine of corruption and oppression.* Unhappily, in the fallen condition of human nature, morality is often held too cheap in the presence of mammon. How many are there who would not hesitate to sacrifice purity, integrity, honour, the highest dictates of duty, for gold! They who would do so are guilty of a crime, but so are they also who would *tempt them to do it.* They who suffer themselves by this means to be drawn into sin are without excuse, but how much more those "by whom the offence cometh!" What an immense amount of iniquity would cease if the stimulus of wealth were withheld; and what an array of moral excellence might we not hope, with the Divine blessing, to see produced, if all the wealth thus rescued from vicious pursuits were devoted conscientiously to the interests of religion! How many a wanderer from the paths of virtue might be reclaimed—how many who are now living abandoned by all sense of shame, victims of a misery all the more dreadful because it is bedizened in present gaiety, waifs on life's highway, soon to be trodden under foot for ever! How many such might be raised to the enjoyments of religion and the blessings of social life! There is a kindred crime which can be perpetrated by wealth alone to which we must refer. It is notorious chiefly in connexion with the exercise of the political franchise, but it is wholly within the province of morals, and has nothing to do with particular principles or parties. We refer to the practice of *bribery*. Hardly any practice can be more pernicious in a public point of view, and none, perhaps, on the character of the individual. It is the besetting sin of wealthy communities, and its unrestrained indulgence is the sure precursor of national ruin. The patriot should denounce it as the most fatal foe to the interests of his country; while the moralist, and, far above all, the Christian should hate it as an egregious violation of the Divine law. God's will should be obeyed in reference to *all* our duties, public as well as private. A people exalted in righteousness will shake their hand from holding of bribes; and of them we may say, "Their place of defence shall be the munitions of rocks," Isa. xxxiii. 16.

The vices to which we have just alluded are confessedly disreputable; a person cannot stoop to them without forfeiting in a certain sense his position with all those whose good opinion is worth possessing; but how many things which the world does not reckon vicious are an abomination in the sight of God! How many methods are there of using wealth which Christ regards with disapproval, which are, nevertheless, adopted without self-rebuke by thousands who bear his name! The Christian church has given munificently perhaps to various evangelical enterprises, but its gifts have been small compared with its possessions. The offerings have been made by the few; they do not represent the concentrated faith and devotedness of the many. Its gifts have been made from its abundance. Alas! how few superfluities have been cut off, how little of privation has been borne, in order to send the blessings of religion and civilization to distant lands! How few economize to give! With what sad unanimity do Christian professors follow worldly men into the paths of extravagant expenditure! The Christian church has yet to learn the scriptural ethics of money. The reader will permit us here to use the words of a "master in Israel." "Let not any man," says John Wesley, "imagine that he has done anything by merely gaining and saving all he can, if he were to stop here. All this is nothing if a man go not forward, if he does not point all this to a further end. Nor, indeed, can a man be said to save anything if he only lays it up. You may as well throw your money in the sea as bury it in the earth, and you may as well bury it in the earth as in your chest or the bank. Not to *use* is effectually to throw it away. If, therefore, you would indeed make to yourselves friends of the mammon of unrighteousness, having gained all you can, and saved all you can, then give all you can. Gain all you can without hurting either yourself or neighbour in soul or body, by applying hereto with unremitting diligence, and with all the understanding which God has given you. Save all you can by cutting off every expense which merely serves to indulge foolish desire, to gratify either the desire of the flesh, the desire of the eye, or the pride of life; waste nothing living or dying in sin and folly, whether for yourself or your children; and then give all you can, or rather give all you have, to God. Do not stint yourself, like a Jew rather than a Christian, to this or that proportion. Render unto God not a tenth, not a third, not half, but all that is God's, be it more or less, by employing all on yourself, your household, the household of faith, and all mankind, in such a manner that you may give a good account of your stewardship when ye can be no longer stewards; in such a manner as the oracles of God direct, both by general and particular precepts; in such a manner that whatever you do may be 'a sacrifice of a sweet-smelling savour' unto God, and that every act may be rewarded in that day when 'the Lord cometh with all his saints.' At this hour and from this hour do the will of Christ; fulfil his word in this and in all things. I entreat you in the name of the Lord Jesus, act up to the dignity of your calling. No more sloth! Whatsoever your hand findeth to do, do it with your might. No more waste! Cut off every expense which fashion and caprice demand. Employ what God has given you in doing good, all possible good, in every possible way, in every possible degree, to the household of faith and to all men." *

We have said that probation is indissolubly connected with every condition in life. Spiritual dangers beset us on every side, and if more numerous in a situation of affluence, they are by no means peculiar to it. The poor man is exposed to perils of his own—perils introduced into his sphere that he may have something with which to wrestle; something to render watchfulness and virtue necessary, and the overcoming of which will confer upon him a degree of blessedness sufficient to compensate for all the toil expended in its acquisition.

The poor man is apt to exaggerate the possession of wealth as a means of happiness. Sensible of many privations which money would remove, his wishes bounded on all sides by the impotence of poverty, he is easily led to imagine that wealth would give him all that heart can wish. Hence he cannot see a wealthy man without instituting a comparison all to his own disadvantage. That individual is in a state all but paradisaical. He need not labour with his hands; no master's eye or factory bell measures to him more accurately than a hour-glass the intervals of relaxation; day after day he may go whither his inclination leads him;

* Wesley's Sermon "On the Use of Money."

his name is a symbol of respect with all classes; he owns a spacious mansion; his eye continually falls on agreeable garden and pleasure grounds—all his own—the very picture of beauty and repose. His rooms are hung with costly paintings; his library is stored with the choicest books; the latest inventions of science stand at his side, as if to tempt the exercise of thought, and render him an epicure in knowledge. Such a man must be happy. Ah! perhaps no other person would be more ready to give the sentiment a flat denial. Perhaps he has often glanced through a rustic lattice, and as he saw his labourer's children gathered round the evening fire, wondered whether the happiness he could not find under his palatial roof had taken refuge there. It is an utter delusion to suppose that happiness is connected with any measure of worldly good. Man's heart is larger than the largest stores of affluence; his wishes never fail to expand in a greater ratio than his possessions, ever increasing the absolute void. His wealth itself is a collection of cares. True happiness lies in doing the will of God; in acquiescing in the Divine arrangements; in cultivating the excellences and discharging the duties of piety. Elsewhere none can be happy, but all may be happy here.

In his demeanour towards those who occupy a higher station, the poor man is prone to errors which reflect dishonour upon himself. Those to which we allude are of two opposite kinds, and candour requires that both should be stigmatized as improper. On the one hand, he may indulge in a mean, slavish, cringing spirit, always speak in a tone more in keeping with the position of a Russian serf than that of a free-born Englishman, and watch every occasion of showing that principle, honour, religion, the most sacred obligations, are secondary in his view to the desire to gratify a rich man's wishes. We know how unpopular such men are with the bulk of their own class; we need not mention here the inglorious epithets which have been coined in order to bring out their conduct in opprobrious relief; sufficient to say that such a spirit is the bane of any population, inimical to morality, perilous to the interests of wealth, the source of pauperism, bribery, and even crime. On the other hand, many of the poorer classes carry their independence to a more rugged and repulsive extreme. They appear to seize every opportunity of saying by their actions to the wealthier employers, "I do not care for you." What a needless, what a dishonourable manifesto! What an exuberance of vulgarity! How rude and low it stamps the character to be of the men who make it! Courtesy and politeness are due from one individual to another. The operative owes respect to all, and therefore, on this general ground, without estimating the obligation which may arise from special relations to his employer, it is a duty he owes himself to be uniformly frank, manly, and respectful;—more, others have no right to ask; less, he ought to be ashamed to give.

The surest safeguard against the moral dangers of every position in life is to be found in the reception of those scriptural truths, which teach us our true relations to God as creatures who, inheriting a depraved nature, have by their transgressions forfeited all claim to the Divine favour, and who, devoid of all merit, can rest their claims for acceptance solely on the atoning sacrifice and righteousness of Christ. This is a view which is calculated to humble pride, and to make the various inequalities of the social condition assume their true level. Scarcely less important also is the duty, when these views have been received into the soul, of maintaining their power by habitually cherishing a prayerful spirit. A prayerful spirit checks the growth of worldliness, allays the turbulence of vanity, and makes a person, even when surrounded with earthly pomp and splendour, walk humbly with God. By maintaining prayer, Daniel was enabled to remain incorrupted at the court of Babylon. Looking at the world in this medium, he beheld its unreality, its evanescence, and discerned the folly of sacrificing piety at the shrine of temporal advancement. In him God gave an illustration of the truth, that they who honour him he will honour. His spirituality was the source of that wisdom which raised him above his rivals, and saved him from the dangers which beset the summit of greatness. Daily humbled and elevated by communion with the King of kings, he could tread the courts of royalty without servility or ambition. If we examine the lives of those individuals who have been equally great and excellent, we shall find that communion with God was the secret of their excellence. They knew the attractiveness of the closet. Business, however pressing, did not engross the whole of their time; they were "fervent in spirit, serving the Lord." Their minds were strengthened by devotion; their judgments acquired greater clearness by being accustomed to contemplate spiritual objects; while, by the same process, they were saved from that absorbing passion for worldly things which often blinds the mind to danger, and conducts it into ruinous errors.

The common excuse for the neglect of prayer is the want of time; but this excuse cannot pass muster with those who find time enough for everything else. In the day most crowded with engagements, what merchant would not find time to confer with a person likely to become a large purchaser? How few would allow a first-rate bargain to slip away on the plea that they had no time to attend to it! It is too evident that such an excuse borrows all its validity from the nature of the duty it is contrived to shun. It would be regarded as insufficient in any case in which our interest or inclination stood concerned: the person has no time for *religion*, no time for the *soul*, no time for *eternity*, though quite enough for everything he truly cares about! But if business is really so extensive as to leave no time for devotion, then business must be curtailed. To a wise and prudent person no other choice would seem to be left. Some time *must* be saved from secular cares to be devoted to our everlasting interests; to the cultivation of spirituality, piety, godliness; to replenish the soul with water from the springs of life. Time thus expended would be time gained. Yes, in sober truth, the separation of a portion of the day for purposes of devotion would be found in the highest degree conducive to the physical, mental, and pecuniary welfare of the man of business. The more pressing his occupations, the more extensive and important his transactions, the more benefit would he draw from seasons of retirement. The closet has no antipathy to the counting-house; the two should go together, just as religion should be allowed to blend with and hallow all the pursuits of life. A clear head is needful in business. A man who will succeed must not allow his brain to be dizzied by a score of plans, all jumbled together in pell-mell confusion. He should see them all in clear outline, as we see a town traced on a sheet of paper, or as a general surveys the field of battle. Some very cool intellects may do this without any moral aid, but devotional habits supply to all the best means of doing it. Few persons comprehend all the bearings of a bargain so well as a disinterested spectator, and he approaches the nearest to such a character who uses the world without being enslaved by it, and in whose mind the interest of present things is properly balanced by the interests of futurity.

One reason why private prayer is so little resorted to by men of business is, that its observance is seldom made a matter of arrangement. It is left to chance, and is generally deferred to the end of the day, when both mind and body are ordinarily so enfeebled as to render it of little use. But this should not be. Independently of evening devotion and that ejaculatory prayer which ought to be interwoven through the whole business of life, a part of the day, in which the mind and body are freshest, should be set apart for communion with God. What season could be more appropriate for this than early morn? What more beautiful than, before the intrusion of worldly cares and temptations, to fortify the mind by the perusal of the Divine word, and supplication for grace to help us in the hour of need? Business is irritating; mistakes, disappointments, losses, are daily occurring to task the temper; how wise, then, before entering upon it, to ascend the mount of celestial fellowship, and seek strength from Christ to honour him through the day! Such a course would make our piety burn brighter, and Christians, through the medium of business, would be the means of recommending religion most powerfully to the common sense and common sympathies of mankind.

CHAPTER VI.

MODELS FOR MONIED MEN: BENEVOLENCE SPEAKING BY EXAMPLE.

WE have spoken of the fallacies and failings of monied men ; but a more pleasing duty remains now for us, namely, the contemplation of money as a talent laid out upon right principles for the service of the Great Creator. The possession of money has been often coveted even by men destitute of religious principles, who recognised it as a powerful instrument for the amelioration of society. How much more, then, must this great talent commend itself to the Christian, as the agency by which his Master's cause may be largely advanced! Let the worldling long for affluence, that he may gratify avarice, sensuality, luxury, political ambition, or a fastidious taste—the Christian blessed with wealth can show him a more excellent way. By the aid of this talent, he knows that he may make war against ignorance, intemperance, ungodliness, and the monster evils that infest society. At home there is disease to heal, modest merit to reward, struggling industry to foster, and above all, the glorious gospel to diffuse. "By money," to use the language (slightly modified) of a vigorous American writer, "he may open a set of books with heaven, becoming the Lord's steward for man's redemption from suffering and crime, laying up his treasures where neither moth, nor rust, nor thieves can approach them. Not a cultured imagination alone, but reason, conscience, religion—all have taught him that the finest and most elegant of all the arts is to paint smiles upon the wan cheeks of suffering infancy; to quench the demon fire of passion that blazes from the eye of precocious wantonness, and kindle in its stead the serene light that radiates from a fount of inward purity; to hang round and pre-occupy the chambers of the juvenile mind with all types and images of loveliness and excellence; and to build up all the glorious faculties, as in colossal architecture, to some nearer resemblance to the Divine original. Reason, conscience, religion—all have taught him that when starving babes shall no longer wail for sustenance upon the starving mother's breast; when blasphemy and obscenity shall no longer be the lullaby with which the intemperate father or mother lulls infancy to sleep; when parental wickedness shall no longer teach falsehood to the youthful tongue, and theft and violence to the youthful hand; when the infinite woes and agonies of earth, which its superfluous wealth and its wasted time might largely prevent, shall cease to be—then may opulence seek its gratification in festivity, or in capricious self-indulgence, without incurring enormous guilt."

Example, however, is by far the best teacher of admitted, but unpractised truths. Lucid statements and powerful arguments may be useful in extending the bounds of conviction, but if the conscience already admits the validity of any precept, then the most effectual method of extending its practical influence is to present it enshrined in some living form. Such a mode of winning attention has many advantages. It is unobtrusive ; it does no violence to prejudice ; instead of taking the garrison by storm, it invites an honourable capitulation. Sometimes a person will be withheld by a feeling of pride from acknowledging himself beaten in controversy, but even pride is disarmed by the voiceless force of example. Some persons are so constituted, that when others point out to them any error, they begin at once to disprove the charge, and will rather continue wrong than consent that another shall set them right. Such conduct is censurable. Surely he who faithfully points out our faults, and helps us to amend them, is our best friend. Even if our bitterest enemy choose to favour us with criticisms on our conduct, provided only he speak the truth, we shall have to thank him for his pains. But example effects its object by avoiding these dangers. Its rebukes are silent; it fights with Socratic weapons, and makes its antagonists their own conquerors.

Happily for the world, it is not yet devoid of great examples. Flattery is hateful, but it is possible to be extravagant in deprecation as well as in praise. Our impression of human imperfection leads us sometimes to speak as if there were no Christian excellence left amongst us; as if the triumphs which Divine grace can win over the selfishness of man's heart were the exclusive trophy of apostolic times; and those heaven-born principles were extinct, which induced the fishermen and publicans of Galilee to "leave all" at the invitation of the Great Teacher, and induced the early converts to sell "their possessions," and count their temporal happiness and wealth but "loss for Christ." But such is not the case. Carping sceptics, who wish to reconcile their real hatred of Christianity with some measure of respect for its Founder, may denounce the religion of the present day as so much ill-disguised hypocrisy; but nevertheless it is impossible to deny the existence amongst us of characters which, though, like everything human, far from being perfect, exhibit a measure of excellence which nothing but religion received into the heart as a vital reality will satisfactorily explain. It is not a boast—of such things God forbid that we should glory!—it is an averment made in sheer self-defence, that Christian men, while falling, and in the estimation of no one more than themselves, far below the standard of holiness revealed in Christ, frequently make sacrifices for the welfare of mankind such as infidelity could never prompt. These sacrifices too are made, not under the influence of any sentiment which could be branded as fanaticism, but by men whom the sceptic is bound to respect; who exhibit in their common life intelligence as extensive, a logic as severe, a shrewdness as all-observant, and a temperament as sober as his own.

Our object, however, is not to obviate the cavils of the sceptic, but to stimulate the Christian to greater excellence, and this we propose to do by bringing to his notice two or three instances of departed worth, which may be the means, perhaps, of keeping before his eye, and thus rendering familiar to him, a standard to which he has not yet attained. It is a salutary employment to muse upon the excellences of those now gone to their reward, till they expand before us into life-like reality. Such visions become our best companions; they accompany us into the crowded city, stand by us in the press of business, speak to us words of counsel audible to none besides, and continually admonish us to follow them even as they followed Christ.

One of the most decisive tests of a person's Christian liberality is afforded by the question —*How much* (not in absolute amount, but as compared with what remains) *does he give to God?* To apply this test, however, it is necessary to recognise clearly the characteristics of Christian benevolence. It is easy to give away a great deal, and give it also to excellent objects, and yet to give nothing *to God*. Here the motive decides all. Christian benevolence springs from a sense of God's ownership in ourselves and in everything we possess. It recognises this fact—God is the sovereign Master of all things; man is but the recipient and steward of his bounty. He whose hand joined cause and effect, endowed us with those faculties which enable us to amass wealth, and constituted that agreement between our organization and external objects which is the source of so much pleasure, can never relinquish his right to the proprietorship of the world. He lays his hand at once on every atom; his omnipotence ever rests in immediate contact with unsentient beings, and secures abstract admiration and entire subservience to his will. Man was intended to be no less under this control, but *his* subjection must be voluntary. What God *enforces* from material nature man must *give*. Bowing with all his possessions at the footstool of Infinite mercy, it is incumbent on him to say—"Lord, I am thine; these also are thine; I can call nothing my own; teach me the duties of my stewardship; let me know what thou wouldest have me do."

The chief motive, however, which induces the Christian to give his property to God is expressed by the apostle in one sentence—"The love of Christ constraineth us." The life of Christ was one sweet, overpowering manifestation of Divine love. His sympathies extended themselves to every form of wretchedness; the poor, the hungry, the diseased, the disconsolate, were the objects on whom he poured the treasures of his compassion; while in the last act of his self-sacrificing career he gave the noblest instance of disinterestedness which the world ever saw. Love to Christ makes us like Christ. There is a transmuting power in love; it is the soul's alchymy; it melts and fuses us into its own pure forms. Christ loved man; this is the chief element of his surpassing beauty; we cannot, therefore, love him without loving man too. Hence love is the soul of Christianity, without which, however vast our knowledge or great our powers, we are but "as sounding brass or a tinkling cymbal." Springing from such motives, Christian benevolence is necessarily distinguished by the *manner* in which it is exercised. Christ prescribed this in one simple rule:—"When thou doest thine alms, let not thy left hand know what thy right hand doeth:" giving for the sake of giving, not for the sake of being *seen to give;* giving from duty, not expediency; a benevolence which would be satisfied if all its gifts were received in the dark, and no subscription list chronicled the name of the giver. But it is by the spirit, not the letter, of this precept that we are bound. True, there is a peculiar charm in the private exercise of charity. How rich a treasure, shut up in the silence of our bosom, is a benevolent action, which has caused, perhaps, the widow's heart to leap for joy, or assisted some one to grapple successfully with difficulties which would else have crushed him! But in many cases such a method of giving is not desirable. Secrecy is not required in order to present a munificent donation on Christian principles, on the contrary, it may be often necessary, for the sake of example, that a gift should be publicly bestowed. In such a case it is a spiritual triumph to give it publicly, and yet feel that no part of the motives flowed from the anticipated publicity. If a person has any apprehension that his heart will be vain of his munificence, it is doubtless advisable in such circumstances to expend it privately; but it would be far better if his principles were strong enough to give publicly, and yet permit him to feel no self-complacency in the act.

It is difficult to prescribe minute rules for giving; we are by no means presumptuous enough to attempt the task. Indeed, is not an OMNISCIENT EYE requisite to fix for each individual how much and in what way he ought to give? Still, there are certain principles of giving which are obviously wrong, and there are certain modes of giving which clearly prove that the principles acted on are those very wrong ones. Who, for example, has not been struck with the uniformity of accounts which characterizes the subscription lists of our religious institutions? Those guineas in "single file," which would lead us to suppose that the donors had been laid on a Procrustes' bed, and their affluence clipped down or extended to the same bulk. But is it so? Should we not often find that one of those guineas proceeded from a purse which could easily have spared a dozen more, while the other perhaps was the offering of a piety so believing and earnest that it set aside the considerations which might possibly have been a justification for giving less? If benevolence always proceeded from true love to Christ, our subscription lists would soon wear a different aspect. There would be less of the contagion of giving, proceeding from without; less desire manifested to "do the same as others," and more of that self-reckoning, conscientious spirit which asks, "How much owest *thou* unto my Lord?" Giving would insensibly become a holier act, fraught with the richest blessings to the giver. An entire change might then take place in the mechanism of Christian effort. Special appeals—appeals so forcible that they leave scarcely anything to the force of inward principle, might then be laid aside. Ease and freedom would be infused into the onward movements of the church of Christ. Instead of impressment, philanthropy would fall back on its army of volunteers. Again, how often do we see uniformity under another aspect—an individual giving precisely the same sum at periods of his life when his circumstances were very different! At the commencement of his career, when yet struggling with slender capital, and the uncertainties of a business not yet established, he gave as much as he gives now after his exertions have long been crowned with affluence. Since that former period how many mercies has he received from the Divine hand!

How many who began the race when he did soon failed, and were snatched away by death from their opening prospects of success, but he has been spared to reap the fruit of his industry! Day after day for thirty years or more he has been kept from fatal accidents, endowed with all but uninterrupted health, crowned with every domestic felicity; his table has been spread with luxuries, his ships have crossed the ocean in safety, his warehouses and factories have been spared the devouring flames; and yet, with such an accumulated debt to the Father of mercies, he gives no more to aid in the diffusion of truth and happiness through the world, than he did when he had not contracted a thousandth part of those obligations. God has placed in the hand of his servant a thousand-fold more wealth than he formerly entrusted to him, but he has spent the increase upon himself, and thus *embezzled* his Master's money. Who can estimate the sinfulness of such a course? It is equally pernicious in its influence on himself and others. It is unjust to his fellow-men whose debtor he is; but it is more than this—it is infidelity to God, who will not fail to institute a scrutiny into the way we have expended the talents entrusted to our care. To be wealthy is to be made God's steward, and for every shilling we are responsible to him.

Thomas Wilson, of Highbury, has left a name which will long be remembered among those who have felt and discharged the responsibilities of wealth. "It was his distinction," says one who knew him well, "to occupy singly, and alone, without all doubt or competition, the first place for usefulness in the denomination to which he belonged. He not only stood alone, but far above others, in that active, liberal, and well-directed zeal on which the prosperity of any cause so much depends. At the age of thirty-four he retired from business. His fortune at that time was not what the world would call *large*, considering his previous position in life, and he appears to have been induced to take that step by a strong desire to devote *himself* to the cause of Christ. Perhaps 'business,' as secular avocations are termed in common parlance, had never been quite congenial to his taste, but this itself was probably owing to the strong bias of his mind towards direct spiritual effort. Such an abandonment of worldly occupations may not be proper in every case; some have felt it a duty to continue in them in order that they might have more to consecrate to schemes of usefulness. We cannot but admire the man who, after having acquired an ample fortune, resolves, instead of retiring into ease and seclusion, to undergo the fatigues of business that he may have more property to consecrate to the welfare of his fellow-men; but it is still more admirable to see a man, like Mr. Wilson, give up business that he may hereafter work exclusively for the spread of religion. Here we see the ardour of his piety—the depth and sincerity of his Christian principles. From the very first it was evident that Mr. Wilson had not abandoned his former pursuits for the sake of ease; he brought into his new avocations all the method, earnestness, and regularity which characterized him in the old. The house he occupied in Artillery-place had only one front room on the ground-floor. 'This,' says his son, 'was used by my father as a place for carrying on his private and public concerns, and was generally called the counting-house, where he sat a great part of the day, devoting many hours to transact what he had determined henceforth to make his business—the happy, joyful business of doing good, and to which he attended with all the energy and vigour which he had learned and practised in his secular calling.'"

It is difficult to estimate the amount of business in connexion with the cause of Christ which Mr. Wilson took into his hands. A mere list of the places of worship which he originated, and the cost of which he in a great part defrayed, would give a surprising view of the extent of his exertions; yet those which he devoted to this branch of labour were but a part of his never-ceasing activity. He was always accessible; always ready to aid by his friendly counsel. He took a lively interest in most of the movements of the day. He was one of the originators of the Bible Society, the Tract Society, and the London Missionary Society. In his post as treasurer of Hoxton Academy, he was indefatigable in promoting the preaching of the gospel. The very year after he undertook the office, two hundred fresh names were added, through his exertion, to the subscription-roll of the institution, and in a few years the number of students augmented six-fold. The objects to which he chiefly devoted himself were those which promised to be most fruitful in spiritual results. Firmly believing in the sufficiency of the gospel, when applied by the Holy Spirit, to regenerate the world, he supported in preference to others those schemes which were most adapted to spread its influence. The good he accomplished in this way is beyond the power of calculation. If his personal exertions are the most valuable and suggestive part of the offering he consecrated to the service of his Master, his benefactions in money were considerable: three enterprises of usefulness in the metropolis alone, undertaken and completed in the course of ten years, cost him £25,000. This munificence is the more striking inasmuch as it was given out of fixed income, and was the fruit of resolute economy. In this point of view his conduct speaks powerfully to others. "To see a man economizing the resources of a handsome, though at the commencement of his useful career by no means an exuberant income, relinquishing the equipage and other appendages of wealth, and contenting himself with the simple habits of men possessed of not half his means, in order that he might have the more to dispense; to see this same man having an office, employing a clerk, and going to the scene of his benevolent occupation, there to be accessible to all who wanted his money or his counsel; and all this with the same constancy, punctuality, and untiring perseverance as any merchant in the metropolis goes to his counting-house, was a scene which perhaps had no parallel, and it still has none!"

THORNTON is an illustrious name in the annals of Christian benevolence. John Thornton was a distinguished merchant, whose chief desire in business, as Mr. Wilson's was in leaving it, seems to have been to lay a richer offering on the altar of his Divine Master. He was a member of the established church, but his love to Christ and his cause was far greater than his attachment to any particular community. Like Mr. Wilson, he devoted a considerable portion of his wealth to the training of young men for the Christian ministry. Among those who were the recipients of his bounty in this form was the rev. John Newton, so well known as the friend of Cowper, and author of the Olney Hymns. A close friendship sprang up between these two excellent men. Mr. Newton became one of his almoners. He regularly received the annual sum of £200 to dispense in works of mercy, and during his entire residence at Olney drew more than £3,000 from the funds of his generous benefactor. His conscientious fidelity in regarding his property as a stewardship is finely illustrated in the following incident:—A clergyman called upon him one morning to receive a promised contribution to some good cause. While waiting in an outer room, he was informed that Mr. Thornton had just received information of a serious failure, involving the loss of no less a sum than £20,000. The applicant could not help regretting his ill-timed visit, and on being introduced to Mr. Thornton, apologized for calling at such a moment. "My dear sir," the latter exclaimed, "the wealth I have is not mine, it is the Lord's, and if He is going to take it out of my hands, it is a reason why I should make good use of what is left." With this remark he doubled his promised subscription. The virtues which distinguished in so eminent a manner John Thornton, descended to HENRY, his third son. The effect of the training he had received under his parental roof were visible in him from his earliest years. At the commencement of his business career, the responsibility connected with the possession of wealth occasioned him much serious thought. He then solemnly vowed that a certain proportion of his entire income should ever after be devoted to the cause of Christ. Throughout his whole life he rigidly adhered to this resolution. While he remained unmarried he gave away six-sevenths of his income, amounting to not less than £9,000 a year, and when he afterwards became the head of a numerous family, his annual benevolence never amounted to less than £2,000. A private account was kept of his various disbursements for charitable objects, proving that he gave on system, and was discriminating as well as liberal. "The poor and needy were not the sole sharers of his income. The fair and reasonable exigencies of those in less humble situation were always met by him with equal generosity and delicacy." The philanthropy he practised was not more striking than the philanthropy which he taught. His house was the resort of men whose names have become eminent in the religious and political world. Wilberforce, Macaulay, Grant, Venn, Gisborne, Simeon, and Henry Martyn, were among his frequent guests, and were accustomed to look up to him with affection and respect. Gifted with a sound and discerning judgment, "he sent his hearers to their homes instructed in a doctrine cheerful, genial, and active—a doctrine which taught them to be sociable and busy, to augment to the utmost of their power the joint-stock of human happiness, and freely to take and freely to enjoy the share assigned to each by the conditions of that universal partnership. And well did the teacher illustrate his own maxims. The law of social duty, as explained in his domestic academy, was never expounded more clearly or more impressively than by his habitual example." But his high and stainless integrity was one of the most striking features of his character. Purer hands, perhaps, were never engaged in the transaction of commercial affairs. He was not only free from many obliquities of conduct which are observed in persons who yet maintain a fair reputation in the Christian world, but he was scrupulous almost to a fault. Information having reached him of the failure of a near kinsman, he was led to inquire how far credit might have been given to his relative, however unauthorized by him, in reliance upon his reputation and resources, and judged it right to cover the liabilities of the defaulter out of his own coffers. A short time before his death, a mercantile house having obtained from his firm without his knowledge large and improvident advances, became so seriously embarrassed that their bankruptcy was urged upon him as the only hope of averting from his own house the most serious losses. He resisted the proposal on the ground that those who had given undue credit had no right to call upon others to divide the loss. To the last farthing he discharged the liabilities of the insolvents, at a cost of more than £20,000. He died in the bosom of a home, says his biographer, which was happy in his presence, from whose lips no angry, morose, or impatient words ever fell—on whose brow no cloud of anxiety or discontent was ever seen to rest.

Normand Smith, an American tradesman, furnished an interesting example of conscientious giving, and in the memorial of his life by Dr. Hawes, his actions yet " speak" to stimulate and encourage others. He was the elder son of a numerous and pious family, thus teaching us the lesson already presented in the case of Thomas Wilson and the Thorntons, that domestic piety is the school of the Christian graces. His business was that of a saddler. His father assisted him with capital at the commencement, but his industry and perseverance soon enabled him to repay the loan. At first his expectations of success were very moderate. To support his family in comfort was the utmost limit of his hopes. Still, while his business was in its infancy and his income small, he set apart a portion for the service of Christ. In doing this he experienced the reward which God has promised to him that soweth plentifully. His business succeeded; at the end of the first year its profits were much larger than he had expected; at the end of the second year they were still greater; the third and fourth year closed with a similar result. Such success would have been eminently dangerous to many men; they would have regarded it simply as an inducement to launch out further into trade, and aim at still greater accumulations. Are there not many who might, with too much reason, date a long career of religious declension from their first prosperous year in business? Not thus was it with Normand Smith. The Christian tradesman may see in him how wealth may be sanctified and made the means of promoting his piety. Finding himself getting rich, he instantly put the question to his heart, What does God intend me to do with my money? The reflections to which he was thus led, resulted in a revival of religious principles and motives within him. He resolved, after making proper provision for the wants of himself and family, to give the rest to the cause of Christ. Like Mr. Wilson, he questioned whether he ought not to leave his business, in order to devote himself more entirely to the service of religion, but the decision to which he ultimately came was adverse to such a step. The spirit which dictated this decision may be inferred from a passage from his journal in reference to it: "The Lord has made the path of duty plain to me. For a year I have been much in doubt as to the duty of continuing my present business. My mind has become settled; I have determined to continue in it, and I trust, not in order to grow rich. I dare not be rich; I would not be rich; they that *will* be rich fall into temptation and a snare. It is my intention to continue in business that I may serve God, and with the expectation of getting to give." This intention he conscientiously carried into effect. Henceforth he was not only "diligent in business," but studiously economical in his expenses—to save money for the cause of Christ.

John Wesley's maxim in reference to wealth was, "Get all you can, save all you can, give all you can." Perhaps the best exemplification of this maxim is to be found in the life of the late Mr. SAMUEL BUDGETT, of Bristol, a member of the denomination which bears the name of that eminent man. The memoir of Mr. Budgett, from the pen of the rev. W. Arthur, is an armoury of counsels and cautions to the man of business. Two lessons in particular may be drawn from it, namely, that rigid justice in *getting* may be combined with bounteous liberality in *giving*, and that the severest application to worldly pursuits may be combined with the most fervent anxiety for the attainment of spiritual blessings. The latter of these is very important. How many believe it impossible to be at once a thorough man of business and a thorough Christian, and that one or the other must be abandoned! This dangerous scepticism is rebutted by a single glance at the life of a man like Mr. Budgett. In the first place, none can deny that he was eminently successful in business. He began his career in the capacity of shopman to his brother, with forty pounds salary—this was his commencement. At the end of three years he was made a partner—junior partner of a small retail shop. In thirty years after we see him at the head of one of the largest mercantile houses in the west of England, turning over nearly three-quarters of a million annually in ready cash. Nor is this result surprising when we consider the man. Enterprise, caution, method, accuracy, punctuality, perseverance, shrewdness; all these elements of the thorough man of business were found in him, so that his success seemed to flow naturally from the exertions he put forth. If any man had "no time for religion," surely it was he. And yet religion was his life; here he found motives to industry, precepts for his guidance, a refreshing stream of comfort and hope, a sphere in which his moral energies might find employment. Religion in him was not a separate faculty; it leavened all his actions and pervaded his whole nature. Business and religion were to him perfectly compatible with each other. His warehouse was a place of prayer; there a spot was consecrated to devotion, and there the master gathered his men around him, and led them in prayer to the Giver of everything good and perfect. How many Christians abandon the prayer-meeting when business grows upon them! Mr. Budgett did not; he was foremost in the means of grace as in the means of wealth, and thus spiritual riches kept pace with his temporal gains. But in the use he made of his wealth we see the most conspicuous illustration of his piety. His liberality in giving surpassed perhaps his diligence in getting. His charity was overflowing. He distributed with discrimination and liberality, and without ostentation, in the estimation of those who were near spectators of his liberality, fully £2,000 a-year. His biographer thinks this too high as an average, but if it was anything approaching that sum, what an example of giving does it place before us! His benevolence had few *crotchets*. It was the offspring of genuine principles. He loved to do good, and in whatever direction it was possible to do this, there he might be found. His generosity was not confined to specially religious objects. To these, it is true, he gave largely. The gospel appeared to him, as it must to all who truly understand it, the one great lever by which mankind are to be raised from sin and its attendant misery, and every organization which was adapted to extend its influence found in him a ready friend. But he appreciated the temporal necessities of those around him, and delighted to alleviate them. During the distress of 1847, he paid large sums in wages to extra hands in order to provide them with food. Many a poor person has he helped by a timely present to surmount the little disasters of humble life, and many more have been indebted to him at the outset of their career for friendly counsel and pecuniary aid. "The successful merchant," the type of a class not unusually the object of envy in the neighbourhood where they reside, was greatly beloved. The interest he took in the welfare of the lowest and roughest of the population led them to regard him with respect. Their demeanour in his presence proclaimed their conviction that he was, in the language of Scripture, "a good man." "Mr. Budgett *was* a neighbour to the inhabitants of Ringwood; thousands of his gold, and thousands of his hours were given for their weal, and to the last his care was for the maintenance of those means of grace which had been so much blessed." He did not pass with unconcern through the uncivilized districts which surrounded the scene of his money-making enterprises. He felt, and justly too, that *there* lay a missionary sphere for him; those men were to be won by kindness and candour to the side of religion; those boys were to be instructed and traine so as to become a blessing rather than a curse to society; those squalid dwellings were to be changed into cleanly abodes by the refining power of example, counsel, and Christian piety. To grow rich in such a neighbourhood, to build up a glittering pile of wealth in the midst of so much ignorance and vice, without laying himself out for usefulness proportioned to his increasing means, appeared to him unworthy of a religious man. He could not do it; at least he *did not* do it. The indefatigable man of business was found working within the shadow of his own residence as the earnest philanthropist, the steady friend of the poor, the originator of every movement by which the temporal and spiritual welfare of his neighbours might be advanced. Oh that such an example were universally followed by our men of wealth! How speedily would many social evils vanish! "The wilderness and the solitary place" indeed would soon "be glad!"

But it is not the wealthy alone upon whom the obligation of Christian benevolence descends; this is the common inheritance of the followers of Christ. Perhaps nowhere are the obligations of giving better illustrated than among those less affluent members of the Christian church with whom an act of generosity is also perforce one of self-denial, who have to economize in order to give. A pleasing instance of this kind may be mentioned as of recent occurrence. Last year, a lady, a member of a church in the metropolis, died, bequeathing

£600 to one of the principal Missionary Societies. The missionary cause had been dear to her. During her life the secretaries of the Society referred to were in the habit of seeing her at the Mission House every six weeks or two months. On these occasions she always had some suggestion to make by which the funds might be increased, and several times in the course of the year brought a sum—never less than £10—as her own contribution. This, the reader will say, was munificent. How many thousands who profess the same attachment to the schemes of Christian piety, and enjoy extensive means, are content to do much less! yet that lady never at any one period of her life possessed more than £60 per annum. "She gave as in the sight of God; she abstained from personal enjoyment to forward his cause; and now, having passed to that heavenly state where all is joy and perfection, one cannot but believe that there must be some stars in her crown reflected from the sanctity of her mode of giving." This is an illustration of what all, to a greater or less extent, may do. Some part of every income, however small, should be set aside for doing good. This should be placed among the common ends of life, to be promoted not by what may be casually left when every other call has been supplied, by the crumbs which fall from the table, but by the first-fruits of our industry.

An instance of exalted Christian philanthropy, more remarkable in some respect than those we have already referred to, is found in the early history of ROBERT and JAMES ALEXANDER HALDANE. These were extraordinary men, endowed with strong mental capacities, and above all, a large-heartedness which led them to devote themselves with burning and inextinguishable zeal to the service of Christ. Their joint lives will be regarded hereafter as marking an important era in the spiritual condition of their native land, and were not without an important bearing on the general progress of the cause of Christ. Robert Haldane inherited the estate of Aithrie, near Stirling, a place of such beauty that a Scotch nobleman rather extravagantly remarked of it, that it was "a perfect heaven upon earth." With an ample fortune and the advantage of a distinguished descent, the world opened to him a career of great promise; but God opened his eyes to behold a better inheritance, and made him willing to count all earthly gain as dross that he might obtain it. Immediately after his conversion he began to feel a deep interest in the spiritual welfare of others. Circumstances directed his sympathies in the first instance to the heathen world. It was the time when Andrew Fuller, on behalf of the Baptist Missionary Society, then recently formed, was delivering his strong and stirring discourses in the churches of Scotland. It is a striking illustration of the usefulness of that eminent man, that his pulpit addresses were the means of determining to such distinguished liberality two such men as Thomas Wilson of Highbury, and Robert Haldane of Aithrie. The subject of missions sank deep into the heart of the latter. He began to think it his duty to go himself to Bengal to labour for the conversion of the Hindoos, and to consecrate his property to the work. He ruminated over the project for six months, mentioned it to his wife, who cordially approved it, and then went to London to confer on the subject with several eminent men whom he was anxious to obtain as colleagues in the work. His plan was to sell his estate, and defray the entire outfit of the mission; then £3,500 was to be given to each minister who should accompany him, as a temporal provision for their families, while £25,000 was to be invested for the future sustenance of the mission. Circumstances finally prevented the carrying out of this design, but the zeal in which it originated proved its genuineness by the works it straightway induced him to undertake at home. In conjunction with his brother, he made Scotland the scene of his missionary labours, and in 1798 sold the estate at Aithrie, that he might have more money to devote to the purposes of evangelization. What a spectacle of primitive simplicity was thus given by these two distinguished men! How full of earnestness and faith was their conduct! "Christianity," exclaimed Robert Haldane, "is either everything or it is nothing;" and in the spirit of this sentiment he spent his life. He expended thousands in spreading the gospel among the population of Scotland, and roused professing Christians everywhere to a truer sense of their duties by the zeal with which he discharged his own. It must be noticed in connexion with these self-denying exertions at home, that he carried the heart and the aim of an apostle into everything he did. It was in consequence of a visit he paid to Geneva that the remarkable revival of evangelical sentiments took place among the students at the university of that city, which led to the conversion of several men of distinguished eminence in after years in the church of Christ, among whom may be mentioned Drs. Gaussen, Malan, and Merle d'Aubigné, the celebrated historian of the Reformation. Thus extensive are the means of usefulness which lie in the hands of a single individual, who anxiously expends the talent intrusted to him in the fear and to the glory of God. What would be the result if similar devotedness were manifested by all the followers of Christ?

We add nothing to these examples. What could increase their power, or augment the eloquence with which they speak to the heart? They bring before us men, not perfect, but men who realized their stewardship, felt they were not their own, grasped the truths of the gospel as everlasting realities, and under the influence of exalted faith brought all they had to the footstool of the Redeemer. They sought not by their liberality or self-denial to establish any claim to the Divine favour. No—the principles from which their generosity sprang were utterly opposed to such pretensions. They had been taught by the Holy Spirit that they were lost and ruined sinners ; quickened by his regenerating influences, they had fled in faith to the Saviour, and rested all their hopes for acceptance on his precious atonement and all-sufficient righteousness. Yielding themselves up unreservedly to the service of Christ, a sense of his love shed abroad in their hearts had constrained them to consecrate all their time, their talents, and their substance, to his glory. May it be the reader's happy privilege to tread in their steps, and to experience the sweetness of an entire surrender of the soul to Him, " who, though he was rich, yet for our sakes became poor, that we through his poverty might be rich!"

APPENDIX.

ORIGIN AND PROGRESS OF SAVINGS' BANKS.

In the main body of our work we have noticed the institution of savings' banks. The merit of inventing these useful depositories for the savings of the poor has been frequently claimed for our own country. The subjoined notice from volume IV. of the Bankers' Magazine, shows however that they were known in other countries before the time of their establishment in Great Britain :—

"It is probable that during the last and present centuries, there have been more public writers whose works have directly tended to attract general attention to the means of ameliorating the condition of the poor than during any previous centuries. No arrangement, however, next to providing employment for the poorer classes, and by it the means of present subsistence, was so important as that affording them the opportunity of husbanding their resources to form a provision against declining age and future necessities. Such an arrangement, at first only partially effected by the institution of the Friendly Societies, would, it was expected by the founders of deposit banks for the safe custody and increase of small savings belonging to the industrious classes, have been completed through the medium of these institutions; but although large sums have been from time to time accumulated in them, the proportion belonging to the poorer classes has, it is feared, been a very small item Among the principal advocates for the foundation and extension of savings' banks, as displayed in their various works on the subject, may be named, Rose and Colquhoun in England; Bernoulli and De Candolle in Switzerland; Krause and Malchus in Germany; and Delessert and Prevost in France.

"It has been stated by a German writer, that the first savings' bank in Europe of which there is now any public record, was established at Berne in Switzerland, in 1787; that about the same time another was established in Geneva; and that in the year 1792, a third was established at Basle. From that period the savings' banks in Switzerland have gone on gradually increasing. As regards England, it appears certain, although there has been some controversy on the subject, that the first institution here, approximating in its character to the existing savings' banks—though on private not national security—was established in the year 1798, at Tottenham, in the neighbourhood of London.

Subsequently similar institutions were founded, namely, at Wendover, in 1799; at West Calder and at Ruthwell in Scotland, in 1807 and 1810; at Bath, in 1808; at Edinburgh, in 1813; and at London and other places in 1816. The dates of the first acts of parliament by which the government undertook at the public expense and on national security the support of savings' banks are the 11th and 12th of July, 1817, and within a few months of that period there were about one hundred savings' banks in England. This number has gone on gradually increasing; and on the 20th of November, 1842—the date up to which the printed parliamentary return on the subject was made up—it amounted to 562 in the United Kingdom.

"It was not until the year 1818 that France imitated the example of Switzerland and England, in the establishment of savings' banks, the first institution of the sort in that country being opened in Paris on the 15th of November in that year.

"Others were very soon afterwards established in the different provinces; and the total number of them on the 31st of December, 1844, was 332, exclusive of the Paris savings' bank and its branches. In addition to Switzerland, England, and France, savings' banks for the poorer classes have been established within the last few years in almost all the other countries of Europe."

That these institutions have exerted a most favourable effect on the temporal welfare of the communities into which they have been introduced, cannot be doubted by any who have attentively considered their effects upon the humbler classes of scoiety.

www.ingramcontent.com/pod-product-compliance
Lightning Source LLC
LaVergne TN
LVHW011222110826
845150LV00006B/1513